T0318194

# Rational Choice

# Rational Choice

Itzhak Gilboa

The MIT Press
Cambridge, Massachusetts
London, England

First MIT Press paperback edition, 2012

© 2010 Massachusetts Institute of Technology

This book was set in Palatino on 3B2 by Asco Typesetters, Hong Kong.

Library of Congress Cataloging-in-Publication Data

Gilboa, Itzhak.
Rational choice / Itzhak Gilboa.
  p.  cm.
Includes bibliographical references and index.
ISBN 978-0-262-01400-7 (hardcover : alk. paper), 978-0-262-51805-5 (pb)
1. Rational choice theory. 2. Social choice. 3. Decision making. 4. Game theory.
5. Microeconomics. I. Title.
HM495.G55   2010
302′.13—dc22                                              2009037119

To my mother, and to the memory of my father

# Contents

**Contents of Online Appendixes**
Available at http://mitpress.mit.edu/rationalchoice.

# Contents

# Preface

The purpose of this book is to introduce readers to some of the fundamental insights of rational choice theory, drawing upon the formal theories of microeconomics, decision, games, and social choice as well as upon ideas developed in philosophy, psychology, and sociology.

I believe that economic theory and its fellow disciplines have provided a remarkable collection of powerful models and general insights, which change the way we think about everyday life. At the same time, economics has been justifiably criticized on several grounds. First, economics is a mathematically oriented field that in many situations fails to provide accurate numerical predictions as do the exact sciences. Second, the basic assumptions of economics have come under attack and have been shown to be falsifiable in experimental studies. Finally, economics is often criticized for failing to deal with important and deep issues such as happiness and well-being, justice and fairness. Moreover, the scientific or pseudo-scientific approach to economics has been argued to be serving the rhetoric of capitalism in a way that may be detrimental to well-being and to justice.

The focus of this book is on some basic insights that survive these critiques. Models of rational choice have been proved sufficiently flexible to incorporate many of the phenomena that economic theory, narrowly understood, fails to explain. These models have also provided important insights into related fields such as political science, biology, and computer science. Touching upon some of philosophy's oldest problems, and benefiting from the use of mathematical tools, the rational choice paradigm appears to be fundamental for understanding the behavior of people and societies, economies and nations, organisms and species. Similarly, it is indispensable for the optimal design of social institutions as well as of automated systems. Accordingly, this book emphasizes the paradigm of rational choice, the general way of thought, the conceptualization, the organizing principles, rather than a particular theory.

Observing the debate about economics and its degree of success as a science, and about the role that economists do and should play in society, one may find biases on both sides. Economists, for the most part, tend to put too little emphasis on rhetoric and the power of the implicit. Most teachers of economics will not say anything wrong about concepts such as utility maximization or Pareto optimality. Yet, they are often unaware of what their students might be reading between the lines, and they are sometimes perceived to endorse what they believe they are only describing. On the other hand, critics of economics often do not retain a sufficiently clear distinction between theory and paradigm. They sometimes flaunt failures of the theory and dismiss the entire field without paying sufficient attention to the merits of the paradigm. I hope this book will make readers aware of both types of biases.

I do not claim to provide a comprehensive list of ideas and insights that may enrich our thinking. The book touches upon issues that appear to me fundamental, useful, and relevant to most readers. I think that everyone should know what's included in this book, and I personally would prefer to live in a society in which every voter understands the issues discussed here. To an extent, this has also been my criterion for inclusion of topics; issues that are too specific or that can be relegated to experts are not included here. Needless to say, even with this criterion in mind, the selection of topics is inevitably subjective.

The book describes material that has been developed in mathematical economics. Most of this material appears in undergraduate textbooks with explicit mathematical models and in graduate textbooks and research papers with considerable mathematical depth. The goal of this book, however, is to distill the main insights and explain them in a language that would be understood by any high school graduate. I attempted to minimize the use of mathematical formulas and professional jargon. If certain paragraphs remain too technical, I hope they can be skipped with no major loss in understanding.

The book has four appendices that may help interested readers understand the issues more deeply but that are not essential for the main insights. They are available online on the book's Web site, http://mitpress.mit.edu/rationalchoice. Appendix A provides a brief introduction to the mathematical concepts used in the other appendices. Appendix B contains a rigorous exposition of some of the material discussed in the book. Appendix C consists of exercises, whose solutions are provided in Appendix D. If the text is covered with these appendices, the book may serve as a textbook for an undergraduate course.

I am grateful to many teachers, colleagues, and students for conversations and comments that have taught and enriched me in many ways. The motivation for writing this book arose from discussions with Hervé Crès and Eddie Dekel. Earlier versions of this book benefited greatly from comments by Daron Acemoglu, Alessandro Citanna, Eva Gilboa-Schechtman, Brian Hill, Barry O'Neill, Andrew Ortony, Marion Oury, and Tristan Tomala as well as from reviewers and editors. I am very grateful also for the bibliographic help and comments of Nira Liberman, Doron Ravid, Arik Roginsky, and Dov Shmotkin.

# Suggested Reading

The text includes some references in end notes. Those are standard references, typically to the first explicit appearance of an idea in the social science literature in the modern era, but they often are not the most accessible or comprehensive sources. Therefore, I list here a few popular textbooks that can be a good starting point for studying the topics in this book. The list is not exhaustive; there are many other excellent textbooks.

## Microeconomic Theory

The following books also cover topics in decision under uncertainty, game theory, and social choice. An asterisk indicates undergraduate level.

Kreps, David, M. 1990. *A Course in Microeconomic Theory*. Princeton, N.J.: Princeton University Press.

MasColell, Andreu, Michael D. Whinston, and Jerry R. Green. 1995. *Microeconomic Theory*. New York: Oxford University Press.

*Pindyck, Robert S., and Daniel L. Rubinfeld. 2008. *Microeconomics*. 7th ed. Upper Saddle River, N.J.: Prentice Hall.

Rubinstein, Ariel. 2006. *Lecture Notes in Microeconomic Theory*. Princeton, N.J.: Princeton University Press.

*Varian, Hal R. 2005. *Intermediate Microeconomics*. 7th ed. New York: W.W. Norton.

## Decision Theory

*Binmore, Ken. 2009. *Rational Decisions*. Gorman Lectures in Economics. Princeton, N.J.: Princeton University Press.

Gilboa, Itzhak. 2009. *Theory of Decision under Uncertainty.* Econometric Society Monograph Series. New York: Cambridge University Press.

Kreps, David M. 1988. *Notes on the Theory of Choice.* Boulder, Colo.: Westview Press.

Wakker, Peter P. 2010. *Prospect Theory for Risk and Ambiguity.* New York: Cambridge University Press.

**Game Theory**

*Binmore, Ken. 1992. *Fun and Games: A Text on Game Theory.* Lexington, Mass.: D. C. Heath.

Fudenberg, Drew, and Jean Tirole. 1991. *Game Theory.* Cambridge, Mass.: MIT Press.

*Gibbons, Robert. 1992. *Game Theory for Applied Economists.* Princeton, N.J.: Princeton University Press.

Myerson, Roger B. 1991. *Game Theory: Analysis of Conflict.* Cambridge, Mass.: Harvard University Press.

Osborne, Martin J., and Ariel Rubinstein. 1994. *A Course in Game Theory.* Cambridge, Mass.: MIT Press.

**Social Choice Theory**

*Feldman Allan M., and Roberto Serrano. 2006. *Welfare Economics and Social Choice Theory.* 2d ed. New York: Springer.

*Gaertner, Wulf. 2006. *Primer in Social Choice Theory.* New York: Oxford University Press.

*Kelly Jerry S. 1988. *Social Choice Theory: An Introduction.* New York: Springer.

Moulin, Herve. 1988. *Axioms of Cooperative Decision Making.* Econometric Society Monograph Series. New York: Cambridge University Press.

# I   Optimization

# 1 Feasibility and Desirability

## 1.1 Examples

**Aesop's Fox**  One afternoon a fox was walking through the forest and spotted a bunch of grapes hanging from a high branch.

"Just the thing to quench my thirst," said he.

Taking a few steps back, the fox jumped and just missed the hanging grapes. Again the fox took a few paces back, jumped, and tried to reach them but still failed. Finally, giving up, the fox turned up his nose and said, "They're probably sour anyway," and walked away.

**Groucho Marx's Club**  "I don't care to belong to a club that accepts people like me as members."

**Wishful Thinking**  "If $P$ is a cause for $Q$, and $Q$ is enjoyable, then $P$ is true."

## 1.2 Separating *Can* from *Want*

These examples should make you smile. The first is a fable dating back to the sixth century B.C.E. It's intended to be more ironic than funny. The other two examples were meant as jokes but also to convey particular messages. These examples have one basic thing in common—they are silly because they involve the confounding of feasibility and desirability, of *can* and *want*.

In the first two examples, what the protagonist wishes depends on what he can achieve. Aesop's fox evidently wanted the grapes. Only when the grapes proved unattainable did he find that he actually had not wanted them, that is, that they were sour and not worth having.

Groucho Marx probably wanted to belong to clubs to be respected and accepted. But then he found he only liked those he couldn't get into. Once a club would accept him, he no longer valued it.

From a psychological point of view, Aesop's fox is much healthier than Groucho Marx. The fox declares that he doesn't want something because he *cannot* have it, whereas Groucho Marx, because he *can*. Thus, the fox brings closer to each other what he wants and what he has, whereas Groucho Marx keeps them apart. The fox may be a caricature of people who are willing to be intellectually dishonest in order to deal with frustration, disappointment, and envy.[1] Groucho Marx makes fun of people who suffer from self-hatred to a degree that does not allow them to be happy.

However, the two examples share the following feature: the feasibility of an option affects its desirability. An option is *feasible* if it can be chosen, if it is possible for the decision maker. The *desirability* of an option is the degree to which the decision maker wants it. Thus, feasibility has to do with beliefs about the world, and desirability with wishes. It appears irrational to mix the two. For example, if you think the grapes are tasty, then they are probably still tasty even if they are hanging higher than expected. If you think that a club is respectable and would be fun to join, then it should remain so after it admitted you. Rationality, we argue, requires that desirability be independent of feasibility.

Wishful thinking refers to considering a state of affairs true only because it is desirable. Assuming that a choice is feasible because we would like it to be is a type of wishful thinking. The sentence, "If $P$ is a cause for $Q$, and $Q$ is enjoyable, then $P$ is true," adds a humorous twist, by giving the statement the general form of a principle of logic such as *modus ponens* ("If $P$ implies $Q$, and $P$ is true, then $Q$ is true"), but it could also be read, "If $Q$ is enjoyable, then $Q$ is true." Again, it seems irrational to judge the feasibility of $Q$ (or $P$) based on how much we like it (or its implications). When we analyze a problem, we should be able to judge what is feasible (possible for us) independently of our goals and desires. Doing otherwise would mean failing to face reality and deluding ourselves.

We are therefore led to suggest that one of the cornerstones of rational choice is a sharp distinction between desirability and feasibility. By sharp distinction we mean not only that the two can be told apart but also that they are causally independent; one does not affect the other.

## 1.3 What Is Meant by *Rational*?

We identified one pillar of rational choice: the dichotomy between feasibility and desirability. This does not imply that examples that violate it, like the ones shown, cannot be found in everyday reasoning. Indeed, these examples are funny mostly because they do remind us of real cases. Moreover, we should be content that there are some real life phenomena that we do not consider rational; otherwise *rationality* would be a vacuous term because everything would qualify as rational.

What precisely is meant by *rationality*? The answer is not obvious. Often rationality is taken to imply the collection of models of individual choice developed in economics. This definition is accepted by most economists, who believe that economic agents can, for the most part, be modeled as rational according to this definition. It is also accepted by most psychologists and behavioral decision theorists, who tend to believe that these models are at odds with the data, and that people are therefore not rational. These two camps disagree on the empirical question of how close economic behavior is to the rational model, but they often agree on the definition of rationality.

I have a personal preference for a different definition of rationality, which is much more subjective. According to this definition, a mode of behavior is rational for a given person if this person feels comfortable with it, and is not embarrassed by it, even when it is analyzed for him. For example, if you don't care for clubs that are willing to accept you, I could point out, "Notice that you wanted this club until they admitted you. You don't care for them *because* they are feasible. Why would you aspire to be admitted by the next club, knowing that you will despise it, too, as soon as you're admitted to it?" I would expect most people to feel uncomfortable with Groucho Marx's choices. That is, I would expect that the separation of desirability from feasibility will be rational for most people. But if someone insisted that they felt perfectly happy with this mode of behavior, I would prefer to think of this mode as rational for them rather than dub them irrational.

The reason I like this peculiar definition of rationality is that I find it useful. An irrational mode of behavior is one that I can hope to change by talking to the decision maker, by explaining the theory to him, and so forth. A rational mode of behavior is one that is likely to remain in the data despite my teaching and preaching. I prefer to think of rationality as a notion of stability, or coherence of the decision with the decision maker's personal standards, rather than as a medal of honor bestowed upon certain decision makers by decision theorists.

According to this view, I present in the next few chapters various ingredients of so-called rational choice, and readers are free to choose and decide which ingredients fit their notions of ideal decision making. It is likely to be the case that a principle of rational choice will be acceptable in some contexts but not in others. My goal in this exercise is not to be convinced that you should make decisions in a certain way, or that most people make decisions in this way, but to enrich your understanding of the choices made by yourself as well as by others.

## 1.4   Uncertainty

Often you do not know whether an option is feasible for you or whether an outcome is desirable. Do these cases result in violations of the separation of feasibility from desirability? The answer is no. Let us start with uncertainty about the feasible options. If I do not know whether I can do something, I can at least *try* to do it, and then the absence of information will be reflected in uncertainty about the outcome of this attempt. For example, I may not know if I can solve a difficult problem, but then I can think of the act "try to solve the problem for two hours," which I can (presumably) choose, and then I have uncertainty about the outcome of this act but not about its feasibility. Thus, there is no difficulty in not knowing whether something is feasible as long as our beliefs about its feasibility are determined independently of its desirability.

Next consider uncertainty about desirability. Suppose that I come to the market at the end of the day. I see only one box of strawberries left for sale. Do I want it? Well, I might suspect that if this is the only box left unsold, there might be something wrong with it. Maybe other buyers have examined it and decided to leave it for a good reason. Of course, I cannot be sure that this is the reason the box is still for sale. But the fact that it is still on the market is a signal about its quality. Taking this into account a priori, I may decide to forgo the trip to the market; if I find anything for sale, it's probably not worth having.

This sounds similar to the Groucho Marx's line. In both cases the decision makers decide not to choose an option because it is feasible. But the similarity is only superficial. In the market example, my preferences about strawberries are inherently independent of the feasible options. In the presence of uncertainty, if I make some plausible assumptions about the behavior of other consumers, I can infer something about the quality of the good from the fact that it is feasible. That is, the link between feasibility and desirability is not a direct causal link; it is mediated by information. Had I known the quality of the strawberries, the fact that they are available for sale would not change their desirability.

In this and the following two chapters, I discuss alternatives whose outcomes are known with certainty. Later, I discuss decisions in the presence of uncertainty. We look first at alternatives that are available to the decision maker but whose outcomes are not necessarily known at the time the decision has to be taken. Then we have to refine the dichotomy between the feasible and the desirable to distinguish among three concepts: feasible, possible, and desirable. The term *feasible* will still refer to what the decision maker can decide to do, whereas *possible* will mean "can happen but not as a result of the decision maker's choice." The term *acts* is often used to refer to the feasible choices of the decision maker, and *states* ("states of nature" or "states of the world") to designate possible scenarios, the choice among which is not under the decision maker's control. This choice will be made by other decision makers or by "nature"—a nickname for randomness or chance—but not by the decision maker herself.

Under conditions of certainty, the emphasis is on the importance of the distinction between feasibility and desirability. Under uncertainty, it will be equally important to distinguish between acts and states, or between feasibility and possibility. Often people arrive at erroneous conclusions when they mistakenly assume that they have control over choices that are not actually theirs to make, or vice versa.

## 1.5   Zen and the Absurd

Is it so obvious that desirability should be independent of feasibility? There seem to be situations in which we wish certain things precisely because they are attainable, or unattainable, and these situations are not as funny as a Groucho Marx line. For example, consider a mathematician who attempts to solve hard problems. She dismisses trivial problems as uninteresting and "not fun" and seeks to solve precisely those problems that have so far eluded her. In this sense, the mathematician would be similar to a mountain climber who seeks to conquer a summit *because* he has not yet done it; or to an imperialist who wishes to add another country to his list of conquests; or to an athlete who attempts to break her own record once more. In fact, we seem to be surrounded by people who seek goals precisely because they may not be attainable and who lose interest in them as soon as they are proven feasible. All of the characters Camus thinks of as "absurd" are of this type.

You may also find reasonable people who tell you that the goal doesn't really matter, it is the road that matters. Zen philosophy might be a source of inspiration for this line of thinking. And if you're interested in the way to a goal rather than in the goal itself, you may prefer a goal that is unattainable. That is, it will be desirable *because* it is not feasible.

Do these examples confound desirability and feasibility? Not necessarily. There are several distinct issues in these examples, and some are simple to incorporate in the standard model of rationality, provided the alternatives are defined appropriately. Suppose, first, that you observe me devouring peanuts. Are you going to conclude that I enjoy having many peanuts in my stomach? Probably not. It will be more reasonable to assume that I derive pleasure from the taste of peanuts rather than from their weight in my stomach. That is, I enjoy the act of consuming peanuts rather than the state of having them. Similarly, I can enjoy swimming in the pool or strolling in the woods without trying to get anywhere.

Next consider a traveler who wishes to visit as many places as possible. He enjoys traveling but derives no pleasure from a daily stroll in the woods. He finds a known place less desirable than a new one. However, he does not seek a new place *because* it may not be feasible to get there; he simply enjoys the discovery, being somewhere for the first time. This phenomenon is also within the scope of rational choice as previously described. As in the case of consuming peanuts, the carrier of utility is the act rather than the final state. Also, in this case the pleasure derived from an act is history-dependent.

The mathematician's example is a little more complicated. As in the case of devouring peanuts, the mathematician enjoys the act more than the state. As in the case of the traveler, the mathematician also seeks the pleasure of a discovery and enjoys the act only the first time. But, as opposed to the previous examples, the mathematician enjoys a solution more, the harder is the problem. That is, she desires a conquest more, the less it appears feasible at first sight. What distinguishes her from Groucho Marx, then?

The answer is not obvious. One may argue that mathematicians, like athletes, enjoy a certain type of exercise and cannot derive pleasure from exercise that requires no effort. According to this account, they do not desire an achievement because it may not be feasible; they simply need to feel their muscles flexed, as it were, to enjoy the solution. Alternatively, you may decide that a mathematician's or an athlete's career is not rational enough for you. As will always be the case, you will make the final decision about what is rational for you.

## 1.6   On Theories and Paradigms

The previous two sections may seem like mental acrobatics. Rather than admitting that the definition of *rationality* involving separation of desirability from feasibility is very restricted, we come up with redefinitions of concepts to save the principle we were trying to promote. Is this honest? And is there anything that could not be classified as rational by some appropriate redefinition of terms?

Theories are supposed to be refutable, and when they are refuted, we should be honest enough to admit that. However, part of the merchandise we are trying to sell is not a specific theory, but a paradigm, a system of thought, a way of organizing the world in our minds. A paradigm consists of certain more or less formal, idealized terms, but, as opposed to a specific theory, it leaves some freedom in the way these terms are mapped onto real life phenomena. Thus, what gives pleasure to the mathematician is flexible enough to be changed from "being able to prove a theorem" to "finding a proof for a theorem that has not been known before."

Throughout this book there are examples of such redefinitions. The rational choice paradigm will often be useful and insightful even when particular theories of rational choice may fail. This is, in fact, why the book is called *Rational Choice* rather than the more common "Rational Choice Theory": in the social sciences it is often hard to come up with theories that are both useful and accurate. But there are many insights and organizing principles that change the way we think about the world. The focus in this book is on the latter.

# 2 Utility Maximization

## 2.1 Example

[*Ann is sitting by a table. Barbara, her sister, enters.*]

*Barbara*:   Hey, what's up?

*Ann*:   Nothing.

*Barbara*:   But you're depressed.

*Ann*:   No, I'm not.

*Barbara*:   C'mon, I know you better than that. You are obviously, positively, definitely depressed.

*Ann*:   I'm not depressed, it's just that....

*Barbara*:   ...yes?

*Ann*:   Well, you won't tell anyone, will you?

*Barbara*:   Of course not, you can trust me; this is what you have big sisters for.

*Ann*:   The same way I could trust you then with the chocolate?

*Barbara*:   Oh, don't be silly, we were kids then. [*Both smile.*]

*Ann*:   Well, the thing is that I have three guys who want to date me, and I can't make up my mind.

*Barbara*:   I see. Well, I have some experience in this matter. Do you like them?

*Ann*:   Uh-huh.

*Barbara*:   All three of them?

*Ann*:   Uh-huh.

*Barbara*:   You're not very selective, are you?

*Ann*: Thank you very much. Why not say, my little sister is so wonderful that she attracts the best guys around?

*Barbara*: Sure, sure, that's exactly what I meant. Anyway, you like all three?

*Ann*: Yes, sort of, you know, there are pluses and minuses, no one is perfect.

*Barbara*: Do you love any of them?

*Ann*: I don't know, I *think* so, I mean I sort of love each of them in some way.

*Barbara*: That means you're not *in* love with any of them.

*Ann*: Maybe. But I still don't want to be all alone. What happens if I'm never in love?

*Barbara*: Okay, here's my idea: you sit down, and attach to each one of them a number. The better the guy is, the higher the number. Then you select the one with the highest number.

*Ann*: That sounds crazy. Did you learn that at school?

*Barbara*: Yes, we called it utility maximization.

*Ann*: Sounds just like the kind of thing that you would study in a business school. How to maximize your utility. Great. Was the course titled "How to use and abuse your boyfriend"?

*Barbara*: Why abuse? What are you working yourself up about?

*Ann*: Just listen to your words: utility, maximization—this sounds so cold, so heartless! Do they also teach you to choose the boy who's richest or whose father is best connected?

*Barbara*: No . . . .

*Ann*: This is love we're talking about, not money! This is about people, and relationships, and emotions, not about stocks and, and . . . . [*She begins crying.*]

*Barbara*: Wait a minute, cool down, okay? First, they do not teach us how to choose boyfriends there; it's a business school, not a summer camp. I was just thinking about this idea because of how we make decisions. Second, I think you're carried away with rhetoric.

*Ann*: Yes, sure, if I don't think you're the greatest genius on earth, I'm carried away with rhetoric.

*Barbara*: No, I mean it, could you give me a chance to explain?

*[Ann is silent, but it's clear she's willing to listen.]*

*Barbara*: And please, without getting overexcited and without attaching meaning to the particular words—that's what I meant by rhetoric: forget about the terms, think about their contents.

*Ann*: OK, I'm listening. But do me a favor, and don't make it as long as last time with the derivatives. I understood nothing.

*Barbara*: Don't worry, this is purely about concepts. And it's short.

*Ann*: Okay, go ahead!

*Barbara*: Think of your choice between any pair of these candidates.

*Ann*: "Candidate"! This isn't politics!

*Barbara*: You see, you get all hung up on the words. What do you care if I call them *candidates* or *choices* or *guys* or *alternatives*?

*Ann*: It's important how you refer to people. Language has an impact on the way we think. You think of them as alternatives, and immediately I start thinking that each of them is dispensable.

*Barbara*: I see your point. In fact, I may even agree with you, for a change. Seriously, I think that what you just said is quite deep. I wonder if economists don't get a lot of unnecessary criticism because of a poor choice of words.

*Ann*: It's not unnecessary. You just agreed that language has its power.

*Barbara*: I meant, unnecessary in the sense that what these economists have to say is actually quite sensible, but because they often choose words that turn people off, people don't listen to what they have to say.

*Ann*: Okay, but I'm mature and open-minded and I'm listening.

*Barbara*: So: consider your choice between any pair of guys.

*Ann*: *Any* pair?

*Barbara*: With three guys you have exactly three pairs. With four guys you would have six pairs, with five, ten pairs, and so on.

*Ann*: You promised no derivatives.

*Barbara*: Derivatives? Derivatives have to do with calculus. This is combinatorics.

*Ann*: You know what I mean.

*Barbara*: Okay, so take these three pairs—think of $a–b$, $b–c$, $a–c$.

*Ann*: I'm thinking of them.

*Barbara*: Would you like to be able to choose between any two?

*Ann*: Yes, of course, that's what I'm trying to do.

*Barbara*: We call this *completeness*. It means that you can always make a choice, that your preferences are *complete*.

*Ann*: And if I find two of them just as good?

*Barbara*: Ties are allowed. You can say that you are indifferent between the two; each is as good as the other. Then you may choose the first that comes to mind, but you won't need to change your choice later on. By the way, it's good for your guys, too.

*Ann*: Huh?

*Barbara*: Otherwise you'd drive them nuts. You'd say yes and no, first you and then him, and then maybe. Do you know, for instance, that Franz Kafka was twice engaged to marry the same woman, and he canceled the marriage both times?

*Ann*: Really?

*Barbara*: Yes, it didn't really make her happy.

*Ann*: Why did he do that?

*Barbara*: Well, he was just incapable of making a decision. The point is there's nothing very romantic about this.

*Ann*: Okay, I get it.

*Barbara*: Good. Now: would your like your choices between pairs to be transitive?

*Ann*: What's that?

*Barbara*: Transitive. This means that if you think that *a* is at least as good as *b*, and *b* is at least as good as *c*, you also think that *a* is at least as good as *c*.

*Ann*: I guess so.

*Barbara*: Sure, you want to make such decisions!

*Ann*: Here we go again. Big wise sister telling Ann what she wants.

*Barbara*: No, no, no, not because I'm your big sister, and not because I'm wise, though both are true.

[*Ann rolls her eyes.*]

*Barbara*: You want to be transitive because otherwise you'll be dating *c* and leaving him for *b*, then dating *b* and leaving him for *a*, and then you'll send *a* away and go back to *c*, and so on, until they're all fed up with you. If you are not transitive, you will be cruel to all the guys involved, and if they have any backbone, you'll be cruel to yourself, too.

*Ann*:  Oh, I thought that being faithful to one means being cruel to all the others.

*Barbara*:  Did I ever say that?

*Ann*:  Da Ponte did, giving this line to Don Giovanni.

*Barbara*:  Oh, good. I was afraid I might have been too honest.

*Ann*:  Very funny.

*Barbara*:  But you get the point—if you want to be neither as indecisive as Kafka nor as fickle as Don Giovanni, you have to be complete and transitive.

*Ann*:  Okay, suppose I am. What wouldn't one do for one's sister!

*Barbara*:  The point is that if you are complete and transitive in your preferences, then it is as if you are maximizing a utility function.

*Ann [suspiciously]*:  Function? This is something with a derivative, isn't it?

*Barbara [smiling]*:  It might have a derivative in calculus. But all I mean is a rule, a way to assign numbers to alternatives.

*Ann*:  What's a way? What is not a way?

*Barbara*:  Just think of a table, where in one column you have the name of the alternative, and in another, the numerical value you attach to it.

*Ann*:  If you mean a table, why do you call it a function? Sometimes I feel you really don't want me to understand what you're saying.

*Barbara*:  I'm sorry. Don't give me this look, I really mean it. The reason it's called a function is that sometimes it will not be given by a table but by a formula. You know, like writing $2x$ instead of listing the value for each and every value of $x$.

*Ann*:  Okay. But I can think of a function as a table?

*Barbara*:  Yes, you can think of it as a table of values that is sometimes more succinctly described by a formula.

*Ann*:  Great. But what did you want a function for?

*Barbara*:  You're so argumentative, I nearly forgot why I mentioned a function in the first place. But I think it's coming back to me. I said that if your preferences are complete and transitive, then I can think of you as if you were maximizing a utility function.

*Ann*:   As if? But I'm not.

*Barbara*:   Well, this is up to you. But let's start by agreeing that this is now only a matter of representation. One can say, "Ann is choosing among her alternatives by maximizing a utility function" and one can also say, "Ann is choosing whom to date in a complete and transitive way, or a decisive and faithful way," and these two statements mean exactly the same thing. It's a mathematical theorem.

*Ann*:   What is?

*Barbara*:   That if you have a preference—a way to compare pairs of alternatives—that is complete and transitive, then it can be represented by a utility function, so that between any two alternatives the one with the higher utility is chosen.

*Ann*:   Always?

*Barbara*:   Well, at least if you have finitely many alternatives. And, pretty as you are, I think that even you don't have infinitely many suitors.

*Ann*:   You're so clever.

*Barbara*:   More than you'd believe. There's even more: not only can I look at you and say, "Ann is maximizing a utility function," without thinking anything bad about you, I can even tell you that finding a utility function and maximizing it is the only method I know that can guarantee that you will indeed be complete and transitive in your preferences.

*Ann*:   So you seriously suggest that I assign a number—call it *utility* if this makes you happy—to each guy and choose the one with the highest number.

*Barbara*:   Yes, that is precisely what I suggest.

*Ann*:   But I really hate the word *utility*. It makes me think of gas, electricity, and cable TV, not of love.

*Barbara*:   Can we call it *payoff*?

*Ann*:   Payoff is what you get when you gamble on horses. Or when you're killed by the mafia.

*Barbara*:   Call it whatever you like. I thought we agreed not to attach too much importance to names. Just assign numbers to your alternatives.

*Ann*:   But I really don't know how I would do that. How do I know if Bob should have a higher number than, say, Jim?

*Barbara*:  Ask yourself, which one do you like better?

*Ann*:  But that's precisely the point; I don't know which one I like better!

[*Barbara is silent.*]

*Ann*:  I mean, this is what you were supposed to help me sort out in the first place, weren't you?

*Barbara*:  You know what? I'll think about it.

## 2.2  Two Points

The example in the previous section illustrates two main points. The first is that terms like *utility* and *maximization* should not turn you off. They do not preclude emotional decision making, love and hate, lofty or base motives. To say that someone maximizes a utility function is merely to say that she is coherent in her choices. Mother Teresa could possibly be described as maximizing the number of healthy children in the world. That is, she maximized a certain function. Adolf Hitler tried to maximize the percentage of Aryan people in Germany. He also maximized a function. Thinking of Mother Teresa and Adolf Hitler as utility maximizers only says that each of them pursued a goal in a coherent way. It does not mean that they are equivalent in terms of ethical judgments, character, or anything of the sort. You are likely to admire Mother Teresa for her utility function and to loathe Adolf Hitler for his. The notion of utility maximization leaves room for all these attitudes.

The second important point, made at the end of the dialogue, is that it doesn't always help to want to maximize a utility function. In the absence of additional structure in the problem, the mathematical equivalence mentioned in the dialogue leaves us no better off than we were when we started.

The dialogue refers to a theorem stating that comparison between pairs is complete and transitive if and only if it can be described by maximization of a function (a utility function). Appendix B provides mathematical details and two formal versions of this theorem. I now turn to the theorem's interpretations.

## 2.3  Interpretations

The theorem in appendix B has three types of interpretations. One concerns normative applications of the theory of utility maximization, namely, applications of the theory recommending modes of behavior to decision makers. The second deals with descriptive applications, that is, with situations in which the theory is interpreted as attempting to describe reality or to predict behavior. Finally, the theorem can be interpreted in a metascientific way, as a way of defining the theoretical terms.

### 2.3.1 Normative

Normative science refers to the activity of scientists, such as decision and game theorists, economists, and political scientists, who address members of an audience and recommend what they should be doing. The audience may be a single decision maker, as in the case of choosing a retirement plan, or a whole country, as in the case of writing a constitution. The main point about normative science is that it's not about describing reality but rather about changing it. Normative science does not try to say how things are but how they *should* be.

Wait a minute, one might think. How does the scientist know? Where does she derive her authority from? Isn't it a bit pretentious to tell people how they should run their lives or to preach to societies what laws they should abide by?

Indeed, a good question. Sometimes people forget what can and what cannot be expected of a social scientist. Let us agree that social scientists are not religious preachers, and they do not have access to any external source of authority. All the social scientist can do is to help decision makers think about what's best for them. Analyzing problems, using general rules as well as specific analogies, invoking mathematical results alongside empirical and experimental findings, the scientist can try to convince decision makers that they would like to make decisions differently than they do. But it is the decision maker who has to make the final choice—the worker who decides on a retirement plan or the country that votes on a constitutional amendment.

If we take the view that the role of the normative scientist is to convince decision makers that they would like to behave in a certain way, what tools does the scientist have? How can she convince others?

In principle, one can use all strategies of debate in order to convince others. But let us assume (perhaps unrealistically) that the scientist has no ulterior motives and that she really wants to do the best for the decision maker. She doesn't want to convince him to buy her software or to keep using her services. She wants the decision maker to be convinced of her teachings and to think, even years later, that he has learned a lot from her. Hence, the scientist does not want to resort to rhetorical tricks in order to win a particular debate; she only wants to use rhetorical tools that provide robust conclusions. Note that I use the term *rhetorical* in a slightly different way than is customary; in this usage rhetoric need not be negative. To be precise, we can distinguish between negative rhetoric and positive rhetoric. Negative rhetoric refers to tricks that may make one lose a debate but for which one has good replies the morning after the debate. Positive rhetoric refers to the type of arguments that make one view the issue differently. Roughly, positive rhetoric consists of devices that you can take from the debate and later use to convince others of what you were convinced of yourself.

Mathematics is such a device. Consider the utility maximization issue again. If a scientist told the decision maker to maximize a utility function, her proposition might appear strange. But if she suggested that decisions be made in accordance with the completeness and transitivity axioms, her recommendation would seem much less controversial, perhaps even trivial. And then the theorem can be invoked to say and prove that whoever agrees with the axioms has to agree with the conclusion as well. It would be very embarrassing to accept the axioms but to reject their implications.

To conclude, the first type of interpretation of the theorem is normative; it can help convince decision makers, ourselves included, that we would actually like to behave in accordance with a particular decision model.

### 2.3.2 Descriptive

Theories in the social sciences are often intended to be descriptions of reality. They provide better understanding of phenomena, and enable predictions, without trying to change reality. This type of interpretation is called descriptive. If this is how we conceive of the theory of utility maximization, what does the theorem teach us? After all, it is an equivalence result. Hence, it does not say anything new about reality; it is just about (the equivalence between) different representations of the same mode of behavior.

Indeed, if a theory makes specific predictions, and it is judged by the accuracy of those predictions, then different mathematical representations of that theory will, by definition, have the same degree of accuracy. But even in the natural sciences, where one can find successful specific theories, theories are selected based not only on their accuracy but also on other criteria such as simplicity and generality. These criteria, among others, do depend on representation. A theory may appear complex in one formulation and simple in another. Similarly, rephrasing a theory may show that it is much more general than previously suspected because in its new formulation it encompasses theories that were thought disparate.

Different representations of the same theory may be even more important when, as in the social sciences, theories often do not provide specific predictions but rather ways of thought and general insights. When we understand theories this way, as paradigms, we find that their degrees of relevance and applicability depend on our intuitive judgment of their plausibility. For example, I later discuss free markets and the reason that economists tend to like them. The argument for the optimality (or efficiency) of the market relies on the notion of utility maximization. If I told you that I believe most people maximize a utility function, you might think I was out of my mind. But if I redescribed the same theory by saying that I believed most people satisfy completeness and transitivity, my claim might appear more reasonable. Thus, the degree to which you believe in the accuracy of my claim depends on how I represent it. The more inaccurate our theories are, and the more we rely on intuition and qualitative arguments, the more important is mathematical analysis, which allows us to view theories in more than one way.

### 2.3.3   Metascientific

Finally, the theorem stated in section 2.2 can be viewed as relating the theoretical term *utility* to the observable term *choice*. This is in line with the logical positivist view in the philosophy of science, which held that the meaning of theoretical concepts is in their observable manifestations. While this view has been criticized within the philosophy of science, it remains a useful guideline in conducting scientific work as well as in everyday life and in political debates. Before we start arguing, it is always a good idea to ask what terms mean precisely. We may find that we are referring to the same thing by different names, or that we use the same word for completely different notions. In our case, the theorem says what is the meaning of *utility*: according to this *revealed preference* paradigm, utility is that function whose maximization is compatible with the choices of the decision maker. This means, in particular, that two utility functions that are equivalent in terms of the observed choices they predict should not be considered different, and we should not waste time and energy trying to decide which one is the correct one.

## 2.4   Measurement Issues

If we think of observable choice behavior as defining the theoretical concept of utility, we can ask, is the utility function that is compatible with the data unique? Or, given certain choice data, can there be different functions that deserve to be called the utility of the decision maker because each of them can provide a description of her choice by utility maximization?

The question of uniqueness arises whenever one attempts to measure a certain quantity. Typically, a measurement function cannot be unique because the unit of measurement matters. For instance, one can measure weight by grams, kilograms, or ounces. It is meaningless to say that the weight of an object is 5 unless one specifies a unit of measurement and gets a more meaningful measure, such as 5 grams or 5 ounces. If one has measurements of weight using grams, one can multiply all numbers by 0.001 and get equivalent measurements of weight using kilograms. Any reasonable theory that can be stated in terms of grams can be restated in terms of kilograms. The same applies to length, which can be measured by meters, centimeters, feet, and so on. Thus, all physical quantities are measured with at least one degree of freedom, namely, the choice of the unit of measurement.

In some cases, we have even more freedom in the choice of the scale. We can choose not only the unit of measurement but also the location of zero. Consider temperature. Fahrenheit and Celsius measures differ not only in the unit of measurement, namely, the meaning of "one degree," but also in the temperature that is called zero. Height of the surface of the earth is another example. We have chosen to measure it relative to the height of the oceans, but we could have chosen a different zero.

When it comes to the measurement of utility, we can hardly expect to be able to have fewer degrees of freedom than in the measurement of physical quantities. We don't hope to be able to say, for example, "My utility from this movie is 6." If we have a function that measures utility, we can multiply it by any positive number and get another function that also measures utility. Moreover, as in the case of temperature, we can probably also determine where to set zero. In other words, given one utility function, we can add a certain number to all its values without changing anything of import. The two types of transformations—changing the unit of measurement (multiplying by a positive number) and shifting the scale (adding a number)—together allow us to take any increasing linear transformation of the utility function in order to get another utility function for the same decision maker. Indeed, it seems natural that the same degrees of freedom that exist in the measurement of temperature will also be present in the measurement of utility.

But with the measurement of utility we have even more freedom than with temperature. If *utility* means "the function being maximized," then any increasing transformation, even if it is not linear, will have the same observable meaning. The utility function that is measured from choice behavior is said to be only *ordinal*: no meaning should be assigned to the particular values of the function; only their *ordering* matters. Thus, if *a* has a higher utility than *b*, and *b* has a higher utility than *c*, we will get the same observable implications if we set their respective values to (10, 1, 0), (10, 9, 0), or (90, 54, 2). The fact that the first alternative can be assigned the number 10 or 90, or that the range of the utility values can be 10 or 88, has no observable manifestations. Similarly, there are no observable implications to the comparison of the utility drop between *a* and *b* versus *b* and *c*. The utility values mean only that the first alternative is preferred to the second, and both are preferred to the third. Any decreasing triple of numbers describes this relation, and therefore any decreasing triple of numbers can be the utility function for this decision maker.

There are other sources of data to help identify a utility function with fewer degrees of freedom. For example, if we expect the function to be used in algebraic calculations, not only in binary comparisons, the family of utility functions that are observationally equivalent shrinks. In chapter 4, I discuss such a theory: the utility function will be used for calculations of expectation, and it will be as unique as the measure of temperature. Alternatively, if we have more data about the probability of choice, we can also pin down the utility function with fewer degrees of freedom. But it is important to recall that utility will typically not be defined in a unique way, and that, in particular, multiplying a function by a positive number yields another function that is, according to most models, observationally equivalent.

## 2.5   Utility and Disutility

It often seems more natural to think of the minimization of disutility rather than the maximization of utility. The two are not necessarily synonymous. Psychology distinguishes between pleasure-seeking and pain avoidance activities. For instance, when you decide which concert to attend, it seems most natural to describe your behavior as utility maximization. By contrast, when you buy a headache medication, minimization of disutility appears to be a more intuitive description of your behavior. Moreover, there are certain patterns of decisions that differ between the two types of activities. It is tempting to think of pleasure-seeking activity as having utility values in the positive range and of pain avoidance as dealing with negative utility values. In such a model, utility will have a meaningful zero, and shifting the utility function by adding a constant will not describe the same behavior. However, it is not clear that the interaction between the two types of motivation can be fully captured by postulating different decision rules in the positive as compared to the negative ranges of the utility scale.

Importantly, data on choice behavior may not suffice to tell whether a problem is one of utility maximization or disutility minimization. When you prefer alternative $a$ over $b$, it is possible that $a$ gives you more pleasure than does $b$, or that $a$ causes less pain than does $b$. Further, there are cases in which the distinction between pleasure seeking and pain avoidance is not obvious even to the individual involved. We eat to satisfy hunger, but we also enjoy the taste of food. We need clothes and shelter to avoid suffering, but we also derive pleasure from them when they are aesthetic and functional.

Thus, the distinction between the two types of motivation is not always sharp and is hard to draw based on choice data. Luckily, in many situations this distinction is not necessary for the description and prediction of choices. If, confronted with the choice between $a$ and $b$, you consistently choose the former, I need not know what drives this choice in order to predict it on the next occasion. For these reasons, classical decision theory does not distinguish between utility maximization and disutility minimization. However, it is useful to bear in mind that in certain problems we may wish to delve into the decision maker's motivation and perhaps treat pleasure seeking differently than pain avoidance.

# 3  Constrained Optimization

## 3.1  General Framework

The discussion in chapter 1 concluded that rational choice should distinguish between the desirable and the feasible. Chapter 2 established that *desirable* means "having a higher utility" for an appropriately chosen utility function. Coupling these two ideas, we are led to a model of rational choice as *constrained optimization*, namely, choosing an alternative that maximizes utility (or an objective function or a payoff function) given constraints.

We may distinguish among three stages in the formulation of a problem:

1. Identify the *decision variables*—which variables are under the decision maker's control?

2. Identify the *constraints*—which combinations of values of the variables are feasible?

3. Specify the *objective*—which utility (disutility) function does the decision maker want to maximize (minimize)?

For example, a firm may find that its decision variables are the quantities of inputs and outputs; its constraints are given by the production technology; and its objective is to maximize profit given market prices of the inputs and outputs. Alternatively, think of a man who tries to lose weight. His decision variables would be the quantities of different foods consumed; his constraints might be ensuring proper nutrition; and his objective minimizing calorie intake.

Schematically, the constrained optimization problem can be written as

max    utility function
subject to
decision variables satisfy constraints

Observe that in a well-defined constrained optimization problem there may be many constraints, which jointly define the feasible set, but only one objective function (a utility function to be maximized or a disutility function to be minimized). Clearly, in reality we often have many goals and many criteria by which to evaluate a decision. But as long as these criteria are not traded off in a single objective function, the decision maker's goals are not well defined. The completeness axiom mentioned chapter 2 requires that the decision maker have preferences between any two alternatives, and these implicitly define the trade-off between different goals.

In real life the distinction between goals and constraints is not as clear as one would like. Suppose that you want to buy a car. You care about the car's performance, price, safety, and so on. In principle, you can buy any car you wish, making your feasible set rather large, and introduce all possible considerations into the utility function. But this requires that you know how to trade off, in a mathematical way, how much safety you're willing to give up for a unit of performance, how much money you're willing to pay for a unit of safety, and so forth. You may find these questions hard to answer. You may even feel that it's simpler to choose the car you like best than to try to specify all these trade-offs mathematically. Indeed, sometimes you know what you prefer without being able to rank all pairs of alternatives or provide a mathematical definition that would apply to all alternatives.

If, however, you are not sure about your preferred choice, you may decide to relegate some of your goals to constraints. For instance, you could say that you require the car to be at least as safe as (specify your lower bound on safety) and then ignore the safety criterion in specifying your utility function. Alternatively, you could demand that the car not cost more than a certain amount and perform at least at a certain level, and then look for the safest car that satisfies these constraints.

If you do relegate some criteria to constraints, does that make them more or less important? Compare, for example, two formulations of the car problem:

(1) max    safety
    subject to    price $\leq P$

and

(2) min   price
      subject to   safety $\geq S$

Which formulation cares more about safety?

The answer is that it depends on the values of $P$ and $S$. If, for instance, $P = \$300,000$, you'd say that the individual in (1) is a safety freak. This individual will probably buy a tank. If, however, $P = \$3,000$, the individual in (1) cares mostly about money and is apparently willing to risk her life quite a bit.

The utility function takes all criteria into account, but it leaves room for compromises. Constraints, on the other hand, are dichotomous: there are no compromises, but once an option satisfies the constraints, the degree to which it does so is immaterial.

The formulation of a decision problem can be a dynamic process in which you look at a given model, contrast it with your intuition, and possibly decide to change its formulation. For example, you may start by thinking that a bunch of criteria are absolutely essential. Say, you look for an apartment and, no question about it, it should be in the center of the city, large, convenient, and inexpensive. Then you find that these constraints leave you with an empty set of feasible alternatives. So you learn to compromise, relaxing some constraints, or moving them into the utility function. For example, you may ask how far from the center you'll have to go in order to satisfy the other constraints.

However, it is important to keep in mind the distinction between feasibility and desirability. It may be useful, in a mathematical model, to designate some criteria for utility as "constraints," but this should only be considered as a heuristic to help trim down the set of relevant alternatives and to simplify the specification of the utility function.

## 3.2   Example: The Consumer Problem

As an example, suppose a consumer can decide how much to buy of each product, as long as his total expenditure does not exceed his income. For simplicity, assume there are only two products. The decision variables are $x, y$, where $x$ is the amount consumed of product 1, and $y$ the amount consumed of product 2. The consumer has an income $I$ and he faces prices $p_x, p_y$. Specifically, a unit of product 1 costs $p_x$ dollars, and a unit of product 2 costs $p_y$ dollars.

Note that this formulation assumes that neither price nor income is a decision variable. Both are on the feasibility side of the equation, so to speak. The consumer may wish to face lower prices or have a higher income, but this would amount to wishful thinking.

Perhaps this is too restrictive. The consumer might have a higher income if he decided to work more. He could also affect the price per unit by deciding to buy large quantities at a discount. He may even affect market prices by his own demand because prices are presumably determined by equilibrium. After all, if all consumers decided to buy more of product 1, the demand for that product would go up, and that might result in a higher price $p_x$. Thus, it does not make sense to assume that no consumer has any effect on the price because this assumption implies that prices do not depend on aggregate demand.

While these objections are not very relevant for the model as an example of constrained optimization, it is worth considering them seriously because that will teach something about the use of models in the social sciences. First, consider income. Indeed, consumers can decide how much to work, and this is a basic issue in the field of labor economics. The standard way to deal with this question is to assume that the consumer's income is given in leisure—24 hours a day—translated to money via the per hour wage. By deciding how much to work, the consumer decides how much leisure she wants to consume: this will be 24 hours a day minus the number of hours per day that she decides to work. Now the model can describe both the choice of the amount of leisure to be consumed and the allocation of the monetary income among the other products. Thus, a model that seems too restrictive for relevant economic phenomena may become satisfactory simply by adding one variable, in this case, by considering leisure as one of the products. This is an almost trivial example of the duality between theories and paradigms. A formal model that may appear inappropriate when considered literally can be recast as a general way of conceptualizing the problem. Applying the same conceptualization in a slightly more general setting makes the model more reasonable.

Second, the model assumes that the consumer has no effect on prices, namely, that she is a price taker. Of course, this is not the case if there are very few consumers in the market under consideration. But in many problems, where there are many consumers and none has too large an effect on prices, this effect can be ignored. This is a bit like solving a problem in physics when one ignores an effect considered to be of secondary importance (say, friction). Whenever we construct a mathematical model for a real phenomenon we make certain assumptions, and these can always be challenged. The question is therefore not whether the model is perfectly accurate but whether it is a good approximation of the phenomenon under discussion.

Finally, consider the issue of quantity-dependent prices due to discounts. It is not clear that this problem can be assumed away as having a negligible effect. Still, we may analyze the model as it stands, see what qualitative insights it provides, and then ask to what extent these insights depend on the unrealistic assumptions we made. Our hope is that some insights and general conclusions will be robust to the unrealistic assumptions. This hope can be substantiated by more elaborate research, testing the model's predictions under more general assumptions. Sometimes, such research will be too complicated to carry out, and we will only make do with intuitive reasoning. In this case we try to focus on the insights that we feel we understand well enough to be able to explain verbally, and independently of the specific mathematical model we started out with. Often researchers feel that mathematical models are only a tool to find candidates for such results and that the mathematical analysis has to be followed by intuitive reasoning, which may sort out the robust insights from those that only hold under very specific assumptions.[1]

## 3.3  Marginality Principle

The marginal utility of a product is the increase in utility that one would get per increase in the quantity of that product. If I consume 100 bananas, and I might consume one more, the utility difference between 101 bananas and 100 bananas is the marginal utility of bananas for me. We can think of marginal utility as the change in utility for a one-unit increase in the quantity, provided that one unit is a small change. If, by contrast, one owns one house and considers buying a second house, one could consider the marginal utility derived from the second house, but this is not what most economists would have in mind when they use the word *marginal*. In fact, the term *marginal* typically refers to an infinitesimal change, and *marginal utility* means the partial derivative of the utility function with respect to the quantity of the product. If the words *partial derivative* are confusing, simply think of a small increase in the quantity of the product, and ask what is the ratio between the increase in utility and the increase in the quantity.

Whether we think of marginal utility in terms of partial derivatives, small changes, or even large changes, we should be willing to accept the fact that this marginal utility depends on the quantities of the products we already have—the product whose quantity we are changing as well as other products. In particular, it is commonly assumed that the marginal utility of a product is decreasing with respect to the quantity of that product. That is, the extra utility one gets from a banana when going up from a quantity of 0 bananas to 1 banana will be larger than the extra utility one gets from the additional banana if one already had 100 bananas. And if you like bananas in a strawberry-banana milkshake, this marginal utility of bananas will also depend on how many strawberries you have. In general, the marginal utility derived from a given product is, like the utility itself, a function of the quantities of all products.

You may recall that we had some measurement problems with the utility function and that it was not uniquely defined. For instance, a change of the unit of measurement amounts to multiplication of the utility function by a positive number. Such a transformation will also change the marginal utilities. Hence, marginal utility is not a well-defined concept as far as observations go. Luckily, there is a marginality principle that does not depend on the actual values of the marginal utilities (with respect to changes in quantities of the different products) but only on their ratios. These turn out to be independent of the particular function chosen.

The marginality principle is a condition, stated in terms of marginal utilities, that is closely related to optimal solutions. It is therefore an extremely powerful tool in identifying solutions. More concretely, under certain assumptions (see appendix B), a solution is optimal if it satisfies the following condition: for each product, *the ratio of the marginal utility to price is the same.*

To see the logic of this condition, let us first write it down mathematically. Let $u_x$ be the marginal utility of product 1, that is, the increase in utility ($u$) following a one-unit increase in the quantity of product 1 ($x$). Similarly, let $u_y$ denote the marginal utility of product 2. The marginality condition is

$$\frac{u_x}{p_x} = \frac{u_y}{p_y}.$$

This condition can be interpreted in economic terms as follows. Assume that I have a tentative allocation of my budget between the two products and that I'm considering buying a little bit more of product 1. Because my budget is fully allocated, this would mean buying a little less of product 2. Suppose I shifted one dollar from the expenditure on product 2 to product 1. How much utility would I lose by consuming less of 2, and how much would I gain by consuming more of 1?

Let us start with product 1. At price $p_x$, one dollar would buy $\frac{1}{p_x}$ units of the product. How much additional utility would I get from this quantity? Since the marginal utility is $u_x$, I can approximate the additional utility of $\frac{1}{p_x}$ extra units by

$$\frac{1}{p_x} \cdot u_x = \frac{u_x}{p_x}.$$

Next, what would be the loss of utility due to the fact that I consume less of product 2? By similar reasoning, spending one dollar less on 2 implies a loss of $\frac{1}{p_y}$ units of product 2. Given the marginal utility $u_y$, the utility loss will be approximately

$$\frac{1}{p_y} \cdot u_y = \frac{u_y}{p_y}.$$

Now, if

$$\frac{u_x}{p_x} > \frac{u_y}{p_y},$$

this shift would pay off: the extra utility derived from one more dollar spent on product 1 would more than compensate for the loss of utility due to that dollar not being spent on product 2. Since this change makes me better off, the tentative allocation I started with could not have been optimal. Obviously, if

$$\frac{u_x}{p_x} < \frac{u_y}{p_y},$$

then it would be a good idea to shift one dollar from product 1 to product 2, and this also means that the tentative allocation could not have been optimal.

Since an inequality in either direction is an indication of a suboptimal solution, the equality

$$\frac{u_x}{p_x} = \frac{u_y}{p_y},$$

that is, the marginality condition, will be helpful in identifying the optimal choice. However, note that certain conditions need to be satisfied for the marginality condition to be sufficient for optimality.

# II  Risk and Uncertainty

# 4 Expected Utility

## 4.1 Examples

**Insurance**  I have a car, which is worth $10,000. I estimate the probability that it will be stolen, over the course of one year, at 1 percent. I can buy insurance, which, for an annual premium of $200, will cover the potential loss. Should I buy this insurance?

The loss is not known, of course. This is a problem under conditions of risk, and the loss is called a *random variable*. It may assume different values (hence it is a variable), but we do not determine its value (hence it is random). Specifically, the random variable "loss" in this example can assume one of the two values, $0 or $10,000 (where "no loss" is captured by a loss of $0). Events will determine which will be the case; the $0 value has probability of occurrence of 99 percent, and the $10,000 value has a probability of occurrence of 1 percent.

One way to summarize the information about a numerical random variable is by computing its *expectation*, a weighted average of all the values it may assume, where the weights are the probabilities. In this case, the *expected loss* is

$$(1\% \times \$10{,}000) + (99\% \times \$0) = \$100.$$

Thus, for each given year, the expected loss is $100, and it turns out that the premium is higher than the expected loss. Does this mean that insurance is a bad idea?

**Lotteries**  I am invited to play roulette at a casino. If I pay $50, I can gain $1,000 with probability 1/37. Otherwise, that is, with probability 36/37, I get nothing ($0). Should I play the game?

Again, compute the *expected gain*, which is

$$\left(\frac{1}{37} \times \$1,000\right) + \left(\frac{36}{37} \times \$0\right) \cong \$27.$$

Clearly, the expected gain is lower than the cost, \$50. Does this mean that I should not play the game?

## 4.2 Expected Value Maximization

In both examples, the answer is no: There is no rule that says, for a single decision problem, that we should maximize the expected payoff. Expectation is a way of summarizing a distribution of a random variable by a number. It is a simple and intuitive measure, but that does not mean that the only rational thing to do is to maximize it.

What does expectation mean, then? We need some preliminaries first. A word of warning: If the next two subsections are too technical, you may skip them. If they are not technical enough, see appendix A.

### 4.2.1   i.i.d. Random Variables

A collection of random variables are *identically and independently distributed* (i.i.d.) if (1) each of them has the same distribution, namely, they can all assume the same values, and they all assume each value with the same probability; and (2) they are all independent—whatever we know about the actual value of any subset of them, we do not have any better guess about the rest; that is, the distribution of each random variable *conditional* on the values of the others is the same as the unconditional, a priori, distribution of this variable.

Intuitively, if we observe a collection of i.i.d. random variables, it is as if we observe a trial or experiment that is repeated *under the same conditions*. Our beliefs about the first experiment are the same as our beliefs will be about the second when it is about to be conducted, and the same is true of the third, the tenth, or the seventeenth. Importantly, the very fact that the second experiment comes after the first experiment and that we will know the outcome of the first when the second starts, does not change our beliefs about the second. This is the independence part. The identicality part is that these beliefs about the second experiment, independent of the result of the first, are the same beliefs as our beliefs about the first.

The concept of i.i.d. random variables is extremely important in statistics. Sampling and statistical inference usually rely on the assumption that we observe variables that are i.i.d. Part of the strength of the concept comes from the law of large numbers (LLN).

### 4.2.2 Law of Large Numbers

The law of large numbers says that if we consider the average of many i.i.d. random variables, this average, which is also a random variable, will converge to their expectation with probability 1. Appendix A explains the exact meaning of the average of the random variables, its expectation, and the statement "with probability 1." The main point is that there is much less uncertainty about the average of i.i.d. random variables than about each one of them in isolation. Even if the variables themselves are rather wild, as long as they are i.i.d. (and not too wild), averaging reduces noise.

The insurance example assumed that each car owner faces a loss, which is a random variable with the following distribution:

| Value ($) | Probability |
|-----------|-------------|
| 0 | .99 |
| 10,000 | .01 |

The expected loss ($) was

$$(.99 \times 0) + (.01 \times 10,000) = \$100,$$

that is, the sum over all rows of the product of the value and the probability. Assume that there are many car owners, and that each of them faces a loss with this distribution and that the losses are independent. That is, whatever you know about the loss incurred by others, you do not change your beliefs about your own loss. Then the more car owners are included in the average, the more confident we can be in predicting that the average loss will be close to $100.

It is not a logical impossibility that the average will be very different from $100. For example, it is logically possible that all insured cars will be stolen, and then the average loss will be $10,000. It is also logically possible that none will be stolen, resulting in an average loss of $0. It is even possible that as the number of cars gets larger, the average will not converge at all. But the probability of all these weird outcomes combined is zero. Thus, we can be practically certain that the average will not be very far from the expectation.

### 4.2.3    Practical Meaning of Expected Value

We can now go back and ask what is the meaning of the expected loss in the insurance problem or the expected gain in the roulette problem.

If we are considering a policy or strategy to be replicated in many identical and independent problems, and if we are interested in the sum (or average) of the payoffs, then we should indeed choose the strategy that offers the highest expected payoff. This is what insurance companies do. Because the insurance company has many clients who presumably face similar and more or less independent risks, the company can be quite confident, thanks to the law of large numbers, that the average claim will be very close to the expected loss. Hence, by setting the premium higher than the expected loss, the insurance company is almost sure that it will make a positive profit. This, however, crucially depends on the assumption that the random variables are, roughly, i.i.d., or, specifically, that they are approximately independent and have similar expectations. For example, if we consider insurance against an earthquake, the claims that may be filed by different clients are not independent. If one claim has been filed, the company can be quite confident that there are others in the mail. In this case the insurance company will still face an aggregate risk, despite the law of large numbers.

Similar logic works for the casino. If it has many clients who are playing the same game in an independent manner, the casino can be practically certain that the average gain will be very close to the expected gain. By charging a participation fee that is higher than the expected gain, the casino is quite sure that it will make money. But this would not be true if, for instance, the casino had only one customer, or if it had many customers all betting on a single spin of the roulette wheel.

The law of large numbers can be viewed as a machine that produces certainty. It does so by taking many random variables and adding them up. If they are independent and identically distributed, the uncertainty about each of them does not accumulate to uncertainty about their average; rather, it washes out, and the average is not subject to uncertainty. However, if there aren't enough random variables involved, or if they are far from being independent, the law of large numbers does not apply. In this case the insurance company and the casino will be facing aggregate uncertainty just like the individual decision maker. And then there is no reason to restrict attention to the expected payoff as the sole decision criterion.

## 4.3   Expected Utility Maximization

In the mid-eighteenth century Daniel Bernoulli suggested that people maximize expected *utility* rather than expected value. That is, he suggested that if we want to predict human behavior, we will do better if instead of calculating the expected monetary value of various choices, we calculate the expected value of a utility function of these monetary values.

Introducing utility into the weighted sum allows much more freedom. Maximization of expected utility can explain many more phenomena than maximization of expected payoff. In particular, the two examples, of insurance and of gambling, are incompatible with expected value maximization but are compatible with expected utility maximization.

Still, it is not clear why people should maximize expected utility rather than some other formula that may or may not involve a utility function. It is also not clear whether it is reasonable to assume that in reality people behave as if they had a utility function whose expectation they were seeking to maximize. The theory of expected utility maximization is more general than expected value maximization, but we may still not be convinced that maximization of expected utility makes sense, whether suggested as a descriptive or as a normative theory.

### 4.3.1   von Neumann and Morgenstern's Theorem

This state of confusion calls for the axiomatic approach. As noted in chapter 2, axioms that relate theoretical concepts to observations can greatly help us in seeing through the rhetoric of a particular theory. For better or worse, knowing what a particular theory, such as expected utility maximization, actually means is necessary for us to judge whether it is a reasonable descriptive or normative theory.

Such an axiomatization was provided by John von Neumann and Oskar Morgenstern (vNM) in the 1940s.[1] They pioneered game theory, in which a common assumption is that when players face distributions over outcomes, they maximize expected utility (see chapter 7). vNM justified this assumption axiomatically. In addition to the axioms of completeness and transitivity, already mentioned in connection with decision making under certainty, they used two more axioms. One is a continuity axiom, which can be viewed as a mathematical necessity. The other, more substantive axiom is called independence. Roughly, it states that when confronted with a pair of two-stage lotteries that have a common component, the decision maker ignores this common component and behaves as if she knew that the common part will not occur. The vNM theorem is formally stated and discussed in appendix B. At this point, it is enough to mention that expected utility maximization is not just an elegant decision rule invented by mathematicians; it has a logic that can be explained in behavioral terms.

### 4.3.2 Uniqueness of Utility

In the context of utility maximization under certainty, I have said that the utility function has many degrees of freedom. It is only ordinal in the sense that any increasing transformation of the function could also be a utility function describing the choices of the same decision maker. For example, if we take all utility values and double them or raise them to the third power, we will get a different mathematical function, but its maximization will have the same observable meaning as the maximization of the original function.

With expected utility maximization the situation is a little different. It is still true that if we double all utility values, the comparison between any two lotteries will yield the same result, but the result might be different if we raise all values to the third power. In fact, part of the vNM theorem is a statement that defines the degree of uniqueness of the function. Once a utility function has been found, one can add to it any number, and multiply it by any positive number, but that's it. For any other modification of the function there will be pairs of alternatives $P$ and $Q$ for which the expectation of the original function is higher for $P$ and expectation of the modified function is higher for $Q$. Thus, if the data include preferences over risky choices, and the expectation of the utility function is used to describe choices, we can measure utility to the same degree of uniqueness as is customary in the measurement of temperature. The increasing linear transformations, which are the type of transformations that relate temperature measured in Celsius, Fahrenheit, or Kelvin scales, are precisely the transformations we can apply to the vNM utility function.

Importantly, if we say that the utility difference between outcome $x$ and $y$ is equal to the difference between $y$ and $z$, this statement has an observable meaning. The decision maker will be indifferent between getting $y$ for sure and getting a lottery that yields $x$ with probability 50 percent and $z$ with probability 50 percent. Thus, the equality between these two differences will have to be respected by any other utility function as well.

It follows that if we try to actually find a utility function for a decision maker, we can choose the utility values of two alternatives arbitrarily, as long as we assign to the better alternative a higher number. It does not matter if these two numbers are 0 and 1, 2 and 17, or −5.6 and 23.5. What matters is only the fact that the second number is higher than the first. The utility values of all other alternatives will be uniquely defined given these two numbers (see section 4.4).

### 4.3.3   Risk Aversion

Consider the insurance example again. We observed that if one is maximizing expected value, one should not buy insurance. This is true whenever the insurance premium is higher than the expected loss. We have good reason to believe that this is generally the case with real insurance policies. The insurance company can rely on the law of large numbers and assume that the average claim will approximate the expected loss. It can then set the premium above that expected loss to cover its other expenses and make a profit. If the insurance company were to set the premium below the expected loss, in all likelihood it would not have enough revenue to cover the claims, let alone other expenses. This doesn't mean that insurance companies always price premiums above expected losses; sometimes they make mistakes in assessing the probabilities involved. But we would expect insurance companies that are still in business not to make many mistakes of this type.

It follows that, for the most part, when we buy insurance we pay more than the expected loss. We behave in a way that can be explained by expected utility maximization but not by expected value maximization. The reason we do it is, presumably, that we do not like risk, and we are willing to pay the insurance company to bear the burden of risk for us. This type of behavior is called risk aversion. More precisely, a decision maker is *risk-averse* if, whenever he faces a lottery with monetary payoffs versus the expected value of that lottery for sure, he opts for the latter. For example, if a risk-averse person is invited to bet $10 on a fair coin, he would pass. He would prefer to get the expected value, $0, for sure rather than gain $10 or lose $10 with equal probabilities. In the insurance example, he would prefer to have $9,900 for sure rather than have $10,000 with probability 99 percent and nothing otherwise ($0 with probability 1 percent). Such a person will typically be willing to get even a lower sum—say, $9,800—for sure rather than doing the lottery.

It turns out that an expected utility maximizer is risk-averse if and only if his utility function exhibits decreasing marginal utility. This means that if he already has $x$ dollars, and one asks what is the extra utility he would get from an additional $1, one would find that this extra utility is lower, the higher is $x$. In technical jargon, the utility function is *concave* (see appendix B).

One may consider the opposite attitude to risk. That is, a decision maker faced with the choice between a lottery and its expected value, she could prefer the lottery. This type of behavior is called *risk-seeking*. It corresponds to a utility function whose marginal utility is increasing, a *convex* function (see appendix B).

When we bet on roulette wheels in casinos, we exhibit risk-seeking (or risk-loving) behavior. We start with an amount of money that is certain, independent of the gamble, and replace it by a lottery whose expected return is lower than that amount of money. How do we know that this is indeed the case? Maybe the expected gain is higher than the cost of participation? The answer is that if this were true, then because of the law of large numbers, the casino would lose money. Since casinos do make profits, it is safe to assume that, for the most part, they offer bets whose expected gain is lower than the participation cost.[2]

If we observe a person buying insurance and gambling at the same time, are they risk-averse or risk-seeking? The answer is not obvious. They may be neither; their utility function may have decreasing marginal utility in some regions and increasing marginal utility in others. It may also be the case that they derive pleasure from gambling that cannot be reduced to calculations of expected utility over the sums of money. To see what the model may be missing, consider the possibility of making the bet much quicker. For example, instead of spending a whole evening at the casino, suppose the gambler gets his net gain as he walks in and then walks out. It seems likely that most gamblers would not find this fun. Typically, they also enjoy the excitement. This means that lotteries over monetary outcomes are inappropriate for describing gambling. The model implicitly assumes that all determinants of utility are summarized in the final outcomes. If a gambler enjoys the process of the lottery itself, this experience should be part of the description of an outcome.

The standard assumption in economics is that people are risk-averse. For many problems one may make the simplifying assumption that people are *risk-neutral*, that is, they maximize the expected monetary value. This is equivalent to maximizing expected utility when the utility function is linear with respect to money. Such behavior can also be viewed as a limit case of risk aversion. Risk-seeking behavior, however, is rarely assumed in economic models.

### 4.3.4  Prospect Theory

There is quite a bit of evidence in psychology suggesting that, at least for descriptive applications, vNM's axioms are violated in systematic ways. Specifically, in their famous prospect theory,[3] Daniel Kahneman and Amos Tversky showed that people tend to magnify small probabilities in their behavior. That is, people react to small probabilities as if they were larger than they are known to be.[4]

A more fundamental deviation of prospect theory from classical economic theory is its claim that people react to *changes* in their levels of wealth rather than to absolute levels thereof. Specifically, it is assumed that the decision maker has a reference point, relative to which levels of wealth are classified as gains or losses. The decision maker may make different decisions involving the same absolute levels of wealth depending on the reference point. Kahneman and Tversky argued that risk aversion is a prevalent phenomenon in the domain of gains, but that risk seeking is much more common in the domain of losses. They argued that loss aversion may dispose people to risk greater losses rather than to settle for smaller losses with certainty.

The distinction between gains and losses based on a reference point is not a violation of an explicit axiom of the classical theory. Rather, it shows that the very language of the classical model, which implicitly assumes that only final outcomes matter, may be too restrictive.

Whereas prospect theory was ignored by economists for a long while, in recent years it has become much more popular. Yet, expected utility maximization is still considered by many to be a good first approximation for descriptive purposes, as well as a compelling theory from a normative point of view. Like any other concrete model in the social sciences, it cannot be a completely accurate description of reality. It may be used to approximate actual behavior, but one should be wary of using it for applications where it has been shown to be a poor model. No less important, we may use expected utility as a tool to derive qualitative conclusions as long as, at the end of the analysis, we return to the assumptions and ask whether the conclusions arrived at depend on the validity of the particular model used.

## 4.4   Elicitation of Utility

Suppose you are asked to choose between two random variables. The probability distribution of one is given by $P$, and the distribution of the second is given by $Q$:

| $x$ ($) | $P$ | $Q$ |
| --- | --- | --- |
| 0 | | .15 |
| 50 | .30 | |
| 100 | .30 | .35 |
| 150 | .35 | .30 |
| 200 | .05 | .20 |

What is your preference between (the random variables whose distributions are) $P$ and $Q$? You probably don't know. It's complicated. $Q$ has 15 percent probability of yielding nothing, whereas $P$ is guaranteed to yield a positive payoff. By contrast, $Q$ has a higher chance of getting the maximum payoff of $200. How would you know which to choose?

The vNM theorem suggests a way. Section 4.3.1 described the vNM axioms only vaguely, but suppose you have read appendix B and accepted these axioms from a normative viewpoint, that is, that you would like to satisfy them; you would prefer to be the kind of decision maker who does not violate the axioms. This doesn't tell you what your choice should be between $P$ and $Q$. There are many ways to satisfy the vNM axioms. In fact, the theorem says the axioms will be satisfied if and only if your choices are consistent with the maximization of the expectation of *some* (utility) function, but it does not indicate which function to choose. Any function will be fine if you want only to satisfy the axioms.

However, the theorem provides quite a bit of structure to help you determine your preferences in simple cases and extend them to complex ones. If you know your preferences between pairs of lotteries that involve only three outcomes, you will have a unique way to define your preferences between any pair of lotteries. Moreover, it is sufficient to know your preferences between sure outcomes on the one hand and lotteries with two possible outcomes on the other. Let's see how this works.

You probably prefer more money to less. In particular, the outcome $200 is better than $0. Looking for the simplest two values for these extreme alternatives, we can set

$$u(200) = 1,$$

$$u(0) = 0.$$

Now consider another outcome, say, $100. It seems reasonable that its utility, $u(100)$, should lie between the two extreme values, that is,

$$0 = u(0) < u(100) < u(200) = 1,$$

but where? Is the utility for $100 above or below, say, 0.5?

There is a simple way to find out. What do you prefer: to get $100 for sure or to get a lottery that gives you $200 with probability 50 percent and otherwise nothing ($0)? The expected utility of the lottery is

$$(0.5 \times u(0)) + (0.5 \times u(200)) = (0.5 \times 0) + (0.5 \times 1) = 0.5,$$

whereas the sure gain of $100 guarantees the utility $u(100)$. This means that its expected utility is also $u(100)$.

If you prefer the lottery, and you are an expected utility maximizer, then your utility function satisfies

$$u(100) < (0.5 \times u(0)) + (0.5 \times u(200)) = 0.5,$$

and if you prefer to get $100 for sure, the converse inequality holds. You may also be indifferent, in which case $u(100) = 0.5$. Notice that in this case the job is done: we have found the value of your utility function for $100.

If we were not that lucky, we can keep trying. If, for instance, you prefer $100 for sure to the lottery, we know that $u(100) > 0.5$. Is your utility for $100 higher or lower than, say, 0.6? All we need ask is whether you prefer the $100 for sure to the lottery that yields $200 with probability .6 and otherwise nothing. If this time you prefer the lottery, $u(100) < 0.6$, and we can continue to compare $u(100)$ to, say, 0.55. If you still prefer the sure gain, $u(100) > 0.6$, and we can then compare $100 to the lottery that yields $200 with probability .7, and so forth. At some point we will find a value $p$ such that you are indifferent between \$100 and getting \$200 with probability $p$ (and otherwise nothing). We can then set $u(100) = p$.

The same value $p$, computed for the sure gain of \$100, will also be used for all lotteries involving \$100, whether they have one, two, or fifteen additional possible outcomes. And when we repeat the exercise for a sure gain of \$50 instead of \$100, and finally for a sure gain of \$150, we will also find $u(50)$ and $u(150)$, and there will be a unique way to rank $P$ and $Q$ in accordance with your reported preferences and the vNM axioms.

The point of the exercise is the following. If you accept expected utility maximization (or the vNM axioms) normatively, that is, you make a metachoice to be one of those decision makers who do not violate this theory, you can build up your preferences in complex choice situations from your preferences in simple ones. Presumably, you have well-defined preferences in some situations. Undoubtedly, you can be confused by increasingly complex problems. The theory can help you extend your intuition from the simple cases to complex ones.

## 4.5   From Simple to Complex

The previous exercise can in principle be done whenever we use axioms normatively. But axioms are more helpful if there is enough structure in the problem to provide a unique definition of the theoretical concept. To see this, compare the previous exercise using the vNM theorem with utility maximization in chapter 2. There, in a dialogue between two sisters, Barbara convinced Ann that Ann would like to maximize a utility function, but at the end of the dialogue Ann wasn't sure whether she had gotten any closer to a decision. There are two related differences between utility maximization (under conditions of certainty) and expected utility maximization (under conditions of risk) that make elicitation a more useful exercise in the latter than in the former.

First, expected utility maximization involves the multiplication of utility numbers by probabilities, the addition of the results, and the comparison of these sums. By contrast, utility maximization only compares numbers. Hence, there is more mathematical structure in expected utility maximization than in utility maximization. Also, in expected utility theory there is sufficient structure for both simple and complex problems, and thus intuition can be extended from simple problems to complex ones. By contrast, in Ann's decision problem all pairwise comparisons were equally simple (or equally complex).

Second, expected utility maximization provides a utility function that is unique up to the determination of two parameters. Thus, we can measure the utility function in one problem, and after it has been calibrated, we can take the unique value that was measured in the simple problem and use it in the complex one. Such an exercise would not have been so simple for Ann's decision problem. There, even if we had fixed certain free parameters, we would have found that a given comparison yielded a set of possible utility functions but didn't pin down a single value for any alternative.

A few comments are in order. First, having a more complex structure is not equivalent to having a unique definition of numerical parameters. We may have very intricate formal models, in which some problems are simple and some are complex, without uniqueness of the parameters involved. On the other hand, even simple models can sometimes uniquely determine certain parameters.

Second, even when there is enough structure to define simple and complex problems, it is not always the case that we have better intuition for the simple ones. For example, suppose you compare life in Paris and in London. The two cities differ on many criteria. Such a problem has enough structure to define simple and complex problems. In particular, one can think of comparisons between hypothetical choices that differ only on one criterion, for example, would you prefer to live in Paris or in a hypothetical Eng-Paris, which is identical to Paris in all respects except that everyone there speaks English instead of French. It is possible that you have clear and well-defined preferences about language that are independent of the other criteria in this problem, and you find this question easy to answer. But it is also possible that you'd say, "I have no idea what Eng-Paris would be like. I find it hard to imagine. By contrast, I do have much more sound intuition for my preferences between the actual Paris and the actual London."

Finally, even without explicit structure in the problem, and even without uniqueness, axioms may be useful in constructing preferences. For example, transitivity can help save some comparisons: if $x$ is better than $y$, and $y$ is better than $z$, we don't need to compare $x$ and $z$.

These qualifications notwithstanding, it is useful to recall that an axiomatization that yields a unique numerical representation can be useful in calibrating the representation in simple problems in order to use it in complex ones.

# 5 Probability and Statistics

## 5.1 What Is Probability?

*Natasha*: I think it's not a good idea to buy an apartment right now.

*Olga*: Oh, yes, why?

*Natasha*: They say that the housing market is going to go down.

*Olga*: Really? For sure?

*Natasha*: Well, not for sure. If they knew this for sure, the market would go down immediately.

*Olga*: So?

*Natasha*: Not for sure, but with very high probability.

*Olga*: How high?

*Natasha*: I'd say, 80 percent.

*Olga*: 80 percent?

*Natasha*: Yes, that's a reasonable estimate.

*Olga*: What does it mean?

*Natasha*: You don't know what 80 percent means?

*Olga*: Don't be silly. I know what 80 percent means. I don't know what *probability* of 80 percent means.

*Natasha*: If you don't know what probability is, I suggest you read appendix A. Ann said that it's all explained there very clearly.

*Olga*: Ann?

*Natasha*: Yes, the girl from chapter 2 who didn't know what a function was.

*Olga*: Thank you very much. I know the mathematical model of probability. My father even studied with Kolmogorov.

*Natasha*:   Kolmogorov?

*Olga*:   Kolmogorov.

*Natasha*:   Whatever. So you know what probability is; it's in your genes.

*Olga*:   Exactly. But that wasn't my question.

*Natasha*:   So? What was your question?

*Olga*:   I'm trying to understand what it means in real life that the probability of the market's going down is 80 percent. What do you want me to understand when you say that?

*Natasha*:   You should understand that it's very likely. It means that it's more likely than unlikely.

*Olga*:   Yes. I see. Sort of, like 70 percent.

*Natasha*:   No, more.

*Olga*:   But 70 percent is also very likely. And more likely than unlikely.

*Natasha*:   I don't understand what you're trying to say.

*Olga*:   I mean I don't understand what's the difference between 80 percent and 70 percent. Of course, I know the difference between 70 and 80 percent of, say, the profit from a movie. But I don't understand the difference between saying that the housing market will go down with 80 percent probability and saying that it will go down with 70 percent probability.

*Natasha*:   Isn't it obvious that 80 percent is more likely than 70 percent?

*Olga*:   Yes, but it's not clear that the numbers mean anything. If you're supposed to give me 80 percent of your profits or 70 percent of your profits, I can check what your profits are and how much you gave me, and see what the percentage is, 70 or 80.

*Natasha*:   Yes?

*Olga*:   Well, I just told you a way to tell whether 70 percent or 80 percent is accurate. But now try to do the same with probability.

*Natasha*:   Okay, go on.

*Olga*:   Suppose one forecaster says that the probability of the market's going down is 70 percent, and another says that the probability is 80 percent. Now you observe the outcome. Suppose the outcome is that the market went down. Which forecaster was right?

*Natasha*: The one who said 80 percent?

*Olga*: But the one who said 70 percent also thought that the market was more likely to go down than not.

*Natasha*: So the one who said 80 percent was "more right" than the other?

*Olga*: Well, I can sort of understand this. But I don't understand the meaning of probability of an event that occurs only once in history.

*Natasha*: How many times can it occur?

*Olga*: I'll give you an example. I work for an insurance company. We sell policies. People pay us money, and if something bad happens to them, we compensate them.

*Natasha*: Hey, I know what insurance is. Even if my father didn't study with Kolmogorov.

*Olga*: Okay, so we try to estimate the probability of something bad happening, say, of a burglar's breaking into an apartment. And we do it by taking the number of burglaries per year, and dividing it by the number of apartments.

*Natasha*: So?

*Olga*: So I understand what probability means. It's the proportion of cases in which something will happen. Or at least has happened in the past. But I don't understand what it means in a single case.

*Natasha*: You mean, like the housing market.

*Olga*: Yes.

*Natasha*: Well, it's sort of similar.

*Olga*: What do you mean? Do you have many housing markets like we insure many apartments?

*Natasha*: Not exactly. We learn from what's going on in other housing markets, but each one is a separate case.

*Olga*: You mean, the market in Russia is not exactly the same as the market in the United States?

*Natasha*: Right.

*Olga*: Let me guess that they are not unrelated either. If the U.S. market goes down, people may start asking questions about the Russian market, too.

*Natasha*: Well, there are differences. The U.S. market may go down without the Russian one going down.

*Olga*:  But one can affect the other. People read newspapers.

*Natasha*:  Of course.

*Olga*:  Well, we don't really have that problem at the office. If one apartment has been broken into, it doesn't mean that another one will or won't be broken into. I can take evidence and use it to estimate probability without worrying that I *changed* the probability I'm trying to estimate.

*Natasha*:  Change the probability?

*Olga*:  Well, I'm not sure. Maybe it's a way to think about it.

*Natasha*:  If you don't know what probability is, how would you know if it changed?

*Olga*:  Okay, maybe not. But you understand what I mean. Estimating the probability of an apartment's being broken into is something I can understand. I understand the difference between 0.2 percent and 0.3 percent. But I'm not sure what you mean when you talk about the probability of the housing market's going down.

*Natasha*:  Do you understand the probability of global warming?

*Olga*:  No, I have the same problem with that.

*Natasha*:  Well, it's a manner of speech.

The notion of probability is ubiquitous. We use probabilities when we discuss risky choice (as in chapter 4), when we deal with the stock market, and with political events. We get the weather forecast in terms of probabilities, and we use probabilities to describe health and environmental risks as well as the outcomes of medical procedures, education plans, and so forth. But what is probability precisely? What do we mean when we say "the probability of an event $A$ is $p$"?

## 5.2   Relative Frequencies as Objective Probabilities

One common answer is the limit of empirical frequencies. When we toss a coin, and say that the probability of heads is 50 percent, one possible interpretation is that if we toss the same coin over and over again under the same conditions, we will find that approximately 50 percent of the times it came up heads. This is referred to as the frequentist approach to probability, defining objective probabilities by limit (relative) frequencies.

This notion might remind you of the law of large numbers (LLN) (see section 4.2.2 and appendix A). Suppose we have a certain trial or experiment repeated infinitely many times. In each repetition, the event $A$ may or may not occur. The different repetitions are assumed to be identical in terms of the probability of $A$ occurring in each, $p$. Also, they are assumed to be independent in the sense that whatever we know about some of them, we get no information about the others. Then the law of large numbers guarantees that the relative frequency of $A$ will converge to its probability $p$.

Note that the LLN relies on assumptions that are defined in terms of probabilities. In saying that random variables have the same distribution or are independent, we presuppose a notion of probability. Also, the statement of the LLN is given in terms of probabilities. Therefore, the LLN cannot be used to *define* probabilities. However, the intuitive definition of probability as "limit relative frequency" turns the law on its head and uses the result of the LLN as the definition of probabilities.

Relying on the intuition of the LLN, we can rephrase this definition of objective probabilities as follows. Assume that we have a large number of experiments that are run under the same conditions. By this we mean that (1) as far as we can tell, the experiments are identical, and (2) the experiments are causally independent—the outcomes of some of them do not affect the outcomes of others. Then, we can take the empirical relative frequency of an event as a definition of its probability in future experiments of the same type.

There are situations, such as the toss of a coin or the shuffling of a deck of cards, in which experiments are run under the same conditions. There are other situations in which experiments are not literally run under the same conditions but may be assumed to be. For example, consider my decision to insure my car. In an attempt to assess the probability of its being stolen, I take the relative frequency of car thefts in the last year as a definition of probability. Indeed, there were many cars that could have been stolen, but only a few were in fact stolen. But were they all identical? Wasn't a brand new luxury car more attractive to thieves than an old inexpensive one? Doesn't the location of the car in the city matter? In fact, no two cars are precisely identical if we take into account all the relevant parameters, such as the car price, condition, and location. Even the assumption of causal independence seems dubious; if two guys are busy stealing your car, they might not have the time to steal mine. It therefore appears that the events in question are neither identical nor causally independent.

Come to think of it, we can make similar arguments about tossing a coin. Even if I toss the same coin over and over again, certain parameters change from one toss to another. My hand may be getting tired. The humidity in the air might change. A comet might change the gravitational field. Causal independence also doesn't seem very plausible; a particularly vigorous toss tires my thumb and increases the temperature of the coin. Similar arguments indicate that in other classical examples, such as rolling dice, spinning roulettes, and shuffling cards, consecutive experiments are never precisely identical or causally independent.

We come to the conclusion that the notion of identical conditions is only an assumption. As is always the case in science, we shouldn't expect assumptions to be perfectly accurate descriptions of reality. It is fine to use models that approximate reality. The wisdom, which is often more a matter of art than of science, is to judge when a certain model is appropriate and when its assumptions are so unrealistic as to become misleading. The same is true of the assumption of identical conditions in the definition of probability. When we use empirical relative frequencies to define the probability of a coin's coming up heads, or the probability of a car's being stolen, we merely assume that the different experiments are practically run under identical conditions.

## 5.3  Subjective Probabilities

In contrast to the previous examples, there are situations in which we can't assume that experiments are identical or causally independent. The result of a medical procedure depends on a host of variables, the combination of which makes each instance unique. The behavior of the stock market also depends on sufficiently many variables to make any day a unique day in history. Moreover, in the case of the stock market, different cases are causally interdependent. This means that if an event occurred in the past with relative frequency of, say, 70 percent, it may now be more or less likely precisely *because* of its past occurrence. A war that is considered a fiasco will render another, similar war less likely to occur. The big financial crisis of 1929 indicates that such crises are possible. But it also resulted in a variety of safety nets that make the occurrence of similar crises in the future less likely. In short, past relative frequencies are not a reasonable definition of probability in many cases of interest.

Still, people often talk in terms of probabilities. The reason is that the machinery of probability theory has been found to be a convenient tool to sharpen our intuition about uncertainty. The need to assign numbers to events in a way that satisfies the basic laws of probability imposes a certain discipline on our thinking. For example, if event $A$ implies event $B$, we can't assign a higher probability to $A$ than to $B$.[1]

When probabilities are defined objectively by observed empirical frequencies, different people who have the same data should, in principle, compute the same probabilities. By contrast, when probability is used only to impose coherence on the quantification of beliefs, we should not be surprised if different people sometimes have different opinions. Their probability assessments are called subjective. The *Bayesian* approach, named for Thomas Bayes, suggests that all uncertainty be quantified probabilistically. If objective evidence exists to suggest a unique definition, as in the case of empirical relative frequencies, we expect rational decision makers to adopt the objectively available probabilities. But if such evidence does not exist, the Bayesian approach still holds that the only rational way to deal with uncertainty is to quantify it by probabilities, even if the resulting probabilities are only subjective.

The notion that probability theory can be used both for objective probabilities (chance) and for the quantification of subjective beliefs has been around from the early days of probability theory (the mid-seventeenth century). The debate as to whether all uncertainty can be quantified by probabilities has been going on ever since, and it seems far from settled.

The Bayesian approach, suggesting that uncertainty can always be quantified and reduced to chance or risk, has received powerful support from axiomatic models. Such a model describes choices under uncertainty, involving events whose probabilities are not known, and suggests a set of axioms on choices, mostly focusing on internal coherence across different decision situations. A theorem is then proved, showing that the axioms are equivalent to the claim that choices can be represented by a certain decision rule—typically, expected utility maximization—that involves probabilities. These probabilities are subjective because they are derived from the decision maker's preferences.[2]

The Bayesian approach can be supported by elicitation schemes that are similar to those discussed previously for the elicitation of utility. Again, the idea would be to start from simple questions and build up toward more complex ones. For example, suppose you are faced with a complicated decision that involves ten different scenarios. You wish to assess your own subjective probability for each scenario. For a given scenario $A$, ask a question of the type, "Do I prefer to get $100 if $A$ occurs or to get $100 if a fair coin comes up heads?" If you prefer to bet on $A$, you may be described as assigning a subjective probability to $A$ that is higher than 50 percent. You can now ask whether you prefer to bet on $A$ or on "at least one head in two independent tosses of the fair coin," comparing your subjective probability of $A$ with .75, and so forth. This way you can calibrate your subjective probability for each event separately and then go on to use these probabilities in more complex decision situations.

There is a claim, however, that betting questions such as these do not have well-defined answers for many events. Asked, "Do you prefer to get $100 if $A$ occurs or to get $100 if a fair coin comes up heads?" I might respond, "Well, you're basically asking me whether the probability of $A$ is higher or lower than 50 percent. But I don't know the probability of $A$; if I did, I would not need your questionnaire anyway!"

Such difficulties have given rise to the development of alternatives to the Bayesian approach.[3] A relatively simple theory that is more general than the Bayesian theory is referred to as maxmin expected utility. It suggests that the decision maker does not necessarily have a unique probability over events but rather a *set* of such probabilities. When faced with a particular alternative, there are many different ways to compute its expected utility because each probability in the set can be used for the calculation, and different probabilities will generally result in different expectations. The maxmin theory suggests that the decision maker tends to evaluate an alternative by its worst case, that is, by the minimal expected utility it can have, where one considers all probabilities in the set. However, this is but one particular theory of non-Bayesian decision making, and many others have been developed.

## 5.4   Statistical Pitfalls

Statistics is used to estimate probabilities explicitly in scientific and nonscientific studies as well as implicitly by most of us in everyday life. It is important to recall that there are several known problems for which we may be led to draw wrong conclusions from available data. The following is a partial list of the types of mistakes that people often make. If you read a daily newspaper, you may try going over the news and asking how many of the headlines lead the reader to make erroneous inferences of these types.

### 5.4.1 Confounding Conditional Probabilities

Suppose you are about to board a flight and you fear the plane might be blown up by a bomb. An old joke suggests that you take a bomb on the plane with you, because the probability of two bombs is really low.

The point of this not-so-funny joke is that, assuming independence of your action and the other passengers' actions, the probability of there being two bombs *conditional* on your bringing one is equal to the probability of one bomb conditional on your *not* bringing one. Quoting the *unconditional* probability of two bombs (brought by other passengers) is an example of confounding conditional and unconditional probabilities.

Another mistake that people often make is confusing the conditional probability of one event given another with the conditional probability of the second given the first. Consider the following example. You are concerned that you might have a disease. You are going to take a test, with the following accuracy: if you have the disease, the test will show it with probability 90 percent; if you don't, the test might still be positive (a false positive) with probability 5 percent. Assume that you took the test and you tested positive. What is the probability that you actually have the disease?

Many people tend to give answers like 90 percent, 95 percent, or something in between. The correct answer is that you have no idea. The reason is that we are only given the conditional probabilities of testing positive given that you are sick and given that you are healthy. But we have no information about the unconditional, a priori probability of being sick. And this information is needed to figure out the conditional probability of being sick given testing positive.

To see this, think about proportions in a given sample of people rather than of probabilities of yet untested cases. Assume there are 10,000 people, of whom 100 are sick. That is, the a priori (unconditional) frequency of the disease is only 1 percent. Within the population of these 100 sick people, the test identifies the disease in 90 cases. Thus, the conditional frequency of testing positive given the sick population is 90 percent. The remaining 9,900 people are healthy. Yet, 5 percent of them will still test positive. This amounts to 495 false positives. Overall, there will be $495 + 90 = 585$ cases of people who test positive. But the sick people among them number only 90. Thus, the conditional frequency of the sick people among those who test positive is only $90/585 = 15.38$ percent.

Translating this back to the language of probability, the probability of testing positive given the disease is 90 percent, but the probability of the disease given a positive test is only 15.38 percent. Note that it is not good news to test positive; before you knew the result of the test, you used to have a probability of 1 percent of having the disease. Given the test, this probability has increased to about 15 percent. Yet, it is much smaller than 90 percent. It is even much smaller than 50 percent. Thus, while the majority of sick people test positive, the majority of those who test positive are not sick.

The relative frequencies we compute in the two cases have the same numerator but different denominators. When we ask what is the proportion of positive tests among the sick, we take the size of the population that satisfies both conditions—the 90 people who are sick and who test positive—and divide it by the size of the population of the sick, 100 people. This ratio, $90/100$, reflects the high frequency of testing positive within the sick population. By contrast, when we ask what is the proportion of sick among those who test positive, we take the size of the same population satisfying both conditions, but this time divide it by the size of the population of those who test positive. The same numerator, 90, is now divided by a different denominator, 585, and the result can correspondingly be very different. Yet, people tend to forget that the denominators are different.

Kahneman and Tversky have documented this phenomenon in careful experiments.[4] They called it "ignoring base rates," because what relates the conditional probability of one event given the other to the converse conditional probability is the ratio between the unconditional (base) probabilities of the two events ($100/585$, in our example). Ignoring base probabilities, or confounding conditional probabilities, is the probabilistic equivalent of the confusion between "A implies B" and "B implies A." Apparently, both are natural mistakes that most of us tend to make unless we are very careful.

Confounding conditional probabilities may also be related to many cases of prejudice about various groups. For example, assume that most of the top squash players are Pakistani. This does not mean that most Pakistanis are top squash players. Yet, the phenomenon we are considering suggests that people often make this wrong implication. And if one replaces this example by something less benevolent, one may find certain prejudices against groups in society that are prevalent but are not statistically justified.

### 5.4.2   Biased Samples

One of the most famous fiascoes in the history of statistics was the prediction of the outcome of the U.S. presidential election in 1936. The *Literary Digest* poll predicted that the Republican candidate, Alfred Landon, would win with a significant margin, whereas in fact the Democratic candidate, Franklin D. Roosevelt, was the winner. In hindsight, people noticed that the poll relied on car and telephone registration lists. Not all voters had cars and phones in 1936, and the sample that resulted was *biased*. It contained a larger proportion of rich people than did the population it was attempting to represent. Consequently, a candidate could have a majority among those sampled but not necessarily among the entire population.[5]

Similar problems may occur if the percentages of poll respondents vary across the relevant subpopulations. For instance, assume that supporters of an ultrareligious party refuse to respond to the pollsters' questions. If the sample is taken at face value, it will underestimate that party's popular support.

These samples were biased because the question of interest happened to be correlated with another phenomenon that affected the probability of appearing in the sample. Some examples involve a bias that is introduced by the sampling procedure itself.

**Family Size**   Suppose I wish to find the average number of children in a family. I go to a school, randomly select several dozen children, and ask them how many siblings they have. I compute the average and take it, plus one (to account for the child sampled), to be an estimate of the average number of children in a family.

A family with five children has a probability of being sampled that is five times larger than a family with one child. A family with no children will disappear from my sample completely. Notice that the bias here stems from my decision to sample children. As opposed to the *Literary Digest* example, to see the bias you don't need to know anything else about the population (such as the fact that Republican voters tended to be richer on average than Democratic voters). It is sufficient to read the description of my sampling strategy to realize that it will result in a biased sample.

Note that the sample is not biased if we want to answer the question, "How many children did you grow up with (including yourself)?" For example, if there are two families, one with a single child and the other with nine children, the average family size is five, but the average number of children living with a child in the same household is indeed $((9/10) \times 9) + ((1/10) \times 1) = 8.2$. Thus, whether a sample is biased or not may depend on the question we are interested in.

**Waiting Time**  I wish to estimate the average time between the arrival of two consecutive buses. I go to the bus stop, measure the time, and multiply it by 2 (to correct for the fact that I might have arrived anywhere over the time interval).

The logic here is similar to that of the previous example. A bus that happens to take longer to arrive has a higher probability of appearing in my sample. If you define "families" of minutes to be intervals between two buses, a minute that belongs to a longer interval has more "siblings."

Observe that the average waiting time in the sample is an unbiased estimate of the waiting time for a passenger who arrives at the stop at a random moment. It is true that such a passenger is more likely to wait for a bus that takes longer to arrive than for a bus that arrives sooner. The sample will be biased, however, if we wish to compute the average over the buses rather than over the minutes.

**The Winner's Curse**  We are conducting an auction for a good that has a common value, say, an oil field, which is worth the same to whoever wins it. This common value is not known with certainty, though. Assume that each firm gets an estimate of the worth of the oil field and submits a bid, and that the estimates the firms get are statistically unbiased (that is, their expectations are the correct unknown value). If only one firm submits a bid, its expected profit is zero. But if more than one firm bids, the firm that wins the bid is likely to lose money.

The reason is that the bids are accurate only in expectation. Sometimes they will be above and sometimes below the correct value. With a single firm, the loss in case it overbid will be offset by the gain in case it underbid, and in expectation it will neither lose nor gain money. But when there are more firms, a firm is more likely to win the auction when it overbids than when it underbids. Thus, when it overbids, it is likely to lose money, but when it underbids, it is likely to gain nothing (because it will not be the one winning the auction).

This is an example of a biased sample. Think of "winning the auction" as a sampling procedure. The bids that are sampled, namely, the bids that win the auction, are not representative of the overall population of bids. As in the previous examples, the bias here in inherent to the sampling procedure.

The winner's curse refers to the phenomenon that the winner of the auction tends to lose money on it. It was observed in practice long ago, and it because obvious that a firm needs to correct its bid downward so as not to lose money in expectation. How the bid should be corrected depends also on what other firms do. In recent decades, game theory has been used to find equilibria in auctions as well as to find optimal auction rules for the seller.

### 5.4.3 Regression to the Mean

In regression analysis we are given data and attempt to find regularities in it. For example, let $x$ denote the height of a man, and $y$ the height of his son. We observe many pairs of values for $x$ and $y$, and ask whether a simple relationship suggests itself. In linear regression we consider only a linear relationship and attempt to find the line that best fits the data points (see figure 5.1).

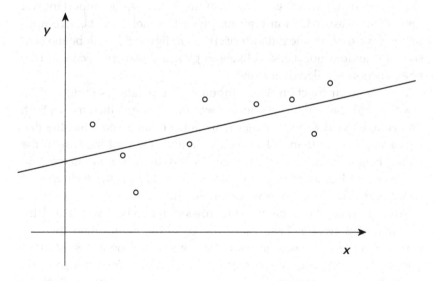

Figure 5.1

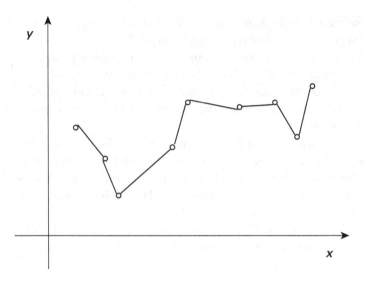

**Figure 5.2**

Why do we look for a simple function such as a line, which will not fit all points, rather than use a more sophisticated function that matches the data more accurately? The reason is that we believe there is inherent noise in the data. In the exact sciences this noise is often referred to as measurement errors. In the life and social sciences the noise also encapsulates many variables that are known to be important but cannot be measured. In any event, given that noise exists, a complicated curve that fits the data precisely (as in figure 5.2) will be too sensitive to random noise and is likely to generate poor predictions. This phenomenon is called overfitting.

When a linear function was computed for the data (as in figure 5.1), it was found that the regression line was increasing, which means that, on average, we'd expect a taller man to have taller sons. But the line had a slope lower than 1 (less than 45°), that is, a unit increase in the man's height resulted, on average, in *less* than a unit increase in the expected height of the son. Because of this fact, the technique is called regression (and not, say, progression).

We can expect the slope of the regression line to be lower than 1 for the following reason. Let's make the plausible assumption that the height of a man depends on his father's genes and on a host of other phenomena, including his mother's genes, his nutrition, and so forth. Without any information on these other factors, let's lump them together into a noise variable and assume, for simplicity, that this noise variable is independent of the father's height.

Let's now pick a particularly tall father, say, the tallest in the sample. This guy probably got to be that tall because of a combination of factors—his genes and his noise variables. Of the two, he will pass on to his son the genes. The noise variable will be sampled afresh by the son. Because the genes do pass on, we would expect the son to be taller than average. But because the random factors are not inherited, we would also expect the son to be shorter than his father. Similarly, markedly short men are likely to have sons who are shorter than average but taller than themselves. This phenomenon is known as regression to the mean.

Regression to the mean is a very common phenomenon. If the variables $x$ and $y$ are measured on the same scale, tend to move up and down together, and a priori one variable can be a reasonable guess for the value of the other variable, the phenomenon is likely to occur. Suppose, for example, that you select students by their grades on an examination and assign the best to a separate class. After a year you check their progress. You would expect them to do better than the average student but also, on average, to be below their previous level. This is simply because of the way you selected them. Having very good grades probably means they have a special talent but also that they were lucky on the day of the exam. You would expect the talent to be a robust trait that will still be there—hence, performance should be above average—but also that the luck component would not repeat itself—hence, performance would drop below last year's.

Imagine that your friend tells you that you simply must see a movie that she just saw. It's the best movie she has ever seen, she says. Regression to the mean should tell you that this is probably a good movie but also that you are likely to be disappointed with the movie given her superlatives.

Unfortunately, the same phenomenon occurs if you rely on your own recommendations. You may be excited about a book or a trip or a restaurant, and wait impatiently to enjoy it again. When you do, you may often be a little disappointed, partly because the freshness of the original experience is not repeated and partly because of regression to the mean.

Other disappointments await us when we select political leaders or investment consultants by their past performance. Clearly, there are some skills that are required to succeed in each of these types of jobs.

We are therefore better off choosing someone who has performed well in a similar job in the past than someone who is a proven failure. But since there is a non-negligible component of luck (noise) in the success of politicians and investment consultants, we should not be surprised that they do not perform quite as well as we hoped when we (s)elected them.

### 5.4.4   Correlation and Causation

Another statistical mistake we are often prone to make is to confound correlation with causation. Two variables, $X$ and $Y$, are *correlated* if they tend to assume high values together and low values together. That is, a high value of $X$ makes it more likely to observe a high value of $Y$ than would a low value of $X$, and a low value of $X$ tends to co-occur with a low value of $Y$. Correlation is a symmetric relation. If $X$ is correlated with $Y$, then $Y$ is correlated with $X$ (see appendix A).

*Causality*, on the other hand, is a much trickier concept. Intuitively, we understand what it means to say that $X$ causes $Y$, or that a high value of $X$ is the cause of $Y$'s taking on a high value as well. We mean something that involves a counterfactual, such as, " $X$ is high and so is $Y$; but had $X$ been low, $Y$ would have been low, too." Causality is not symmetric. If $X$ is a cause of $Y$, $Y$ cannot be a cause of $X$ .Specifically, if $X$ is a cause of $Y$, it has to happen before $Y$. It is possible that a high value of $X$ today is the cause of a high value of $Y$ tomorrow and that the latter is in turn the cause of a high value of $X$ the following day. Yet, a high value of $Y$ tomorrow cannot be the cause of a high value of $X$ today. Correlation need not respect temporal precedence. A high value of $Y$ tomorrow may be correlated with, or may be an indication of, a high value of $X$ today. But the former cannot be the cause of the latter because causality does respect temporal precedence.

Causality is harder to define, measure, and establish than correlation because causality involves counterfactual statements such as "had $X$ been low, $Y$ would have been low, too." The basic problem is that it is not always clear what would have happened if $X$ had taken on a different value than it did in reality. To consider an extreme example, we can think of causality in history. What were the causes of Hitler's defeat? Would he have won the war if he had not attacked the USSR? And what were the causes of the collapse of the Soviet Union? Would the USSR have survived were it not for the "star wars" project? or the decline in the price of oil? We do not know the answers to these questions. It is hard to give exact conditions under which the answer should be yes or no because we cannot rerun history and check what would have happened under different circumstances.

Historical events are an extreme example because they tend to be unique. When every two events differ from each other in a multitude of observable features, it is difficult to define correlation, let alone causality. But even when we have sufficiently similar repetitions of events to define correlation, causality may still be elusive. The reason is that a given correlation is compatible with many causal stories. For example, assume there is a correlation between income, $X$, and expenditure on a car, $Y$. This statistical relation may be a result of (1) $X$ being the cause of $Y$, (2) $Y$ being the cause of $X$, (3) a causal relation that does not directly relate $X$ and $Y$, for instance, another variable, $Z$, may be the cause of both $X$ and $Y$, and (4) pure chance.

There are statistical inference techniques that are designed to rule out the last case, pure chance. The notion of statistical significance attempts to distinguish the fundamental relationships from those that just happened to reveal themselves in the data due to sampling errors. But the correlation between $X$ and $Y$ can be statistically significant in any of the cases (1)–(3).

Fortunately, if we just want to learn things about the world, we need not worry about causality. If we see a person who owns an expensive car, we may conclude that she is more likely to be rich than if she owned an inexpensive car. This would be a valid statistical inference even if we believed that causation goes the other way around, namely, that she bought an expensive car because she could afford it.

Unfortunately, if we wish to study relationships among phenomena in order to change things in the world, we do need to establish causal relationships. If you want to have an expensive car, it makes sense that you should try to get rich. But it would probably be a bad idea to buy an expensive car in the hope that you will thereby become rich.

There are many examples in which common sense may ensure that we do not confuse correlation with causation. Being sick is correlated with seeing doctors, but we are unlikely to mistake the doctors as the main cause of diseases. Taller children tend to have taller parents, but it is clear that the height of the child is not the cause of the height of the parent. To consider examples with more than two variables, we may find that the population sizes in Greece and in Argentina are correlated (over different years), and this may be a result of both populations growing with time. Such a spurious correlation results from two causal relationships but does not convey a causal relationship itself. Spurious correlations will disappear once we control for the relevant variables. If we take into account the time variable, we will find that *given* the effect of this variable, the other two variables are not correlated.

But there are examples in which the causal relationships are not so obvious. Suppose a study finds that a little bit of smoking is related to diseases less than not smoking at all, and only at high levels of nicotine consumption are negative health effects observed. One might suspect that some smoking is actually good for us. (Indeed, this is allegedly the case with red wine.) But it may also be the case that the population of nonsmokers includes those people who are already sick and who were ordered by their doctors to stop smoking. In this case, the sick nonsmokers do not smoke because they are sick rather than the other way around.

If we find that children's verbal abilities are related to their height, we are unlikely to stretch children in the hope of making them more verbal. We will probably realize that age must be the common factor that causes both an increase in height and in verbal abilities. In this case, common sense helps rule out a direct causal link between height and verbal skills. But if we find that children of richer parents do better in school, we may find it hard to judge which causal theory makes more sense: it is possible that more money allows better education but also that people who are a priori more talented tend to have more money as well as more talented children.

How can we establish causal relationships? If we know which variables are suspected of mediating a correlation between $X$ and $Y$ and which may be common causes of both (such as the parents' talent in the last example), we can include them in the analysis and see if correlation persists. If the correlation between $X$ and $Y$ is there given the same value of a suspected variable $Z$, then this variable is probably not the cause of $Y$.

But how many variables should we consider? There may be no end to the possible causes of a given phenomenon. It is therefore desirable to have controlled experiments, in which one can change the value of only one variable, $X$, and see its effect on another, $Y$. If the assignment of cases to the groups of different $X$ values is random, and different values of $Y$ result, one feels that a causal relationship has been established. The trick about random assignment is that another variable $Z$ that we should have controlled for has the same distribution in the various groups (defined by $X$ values). For example, if I wish to test the efficacy of a new learning program, and I can assign students to different groups at random, a significant difference in their performance at the end can only be attributed to the learning program to which they were assigned.

There are many situations, however, in which controlled experiments are impossible, impractical, or unethical. History is one example in which experiments are theoretically impossible. We cannot rebuild the Soviet Union and see what might bring its disintegration, if only because the memory of the first event changes the second one. Moreover, any experiment that involves a whole country, society, or economy will typically not be practical. Practical experiments also need to end in a reasonable time. Finding out the effects of a certain education system on future performance of children might require an experiment that takes, say, 40 years. By the time it is done, it will probably not be relevant any longer. Finally, ethical constraints abound. Suppose, for example, that we're not sure whether pregnant women can drink a little bit of wine without harm. We can't take a sample of pregnant women and randomly tell half of them to drink while the others don't, in order to see which group produces children with more birth defects.

There are more sophisticated statistical techniques that are designed to identify causation based on naturally available data. But they are limited, and leave unanswered many causal questions in macroeconomics and finance, political science, sociology, and so forth. Moreover, many statistical correlations are reported without further analysis. It is therefore important, when consuming statistical data, to bear in mind that correlation does not imply causation.

### 5.4.5  Statistical Significance
The standard way that facts are statistically proven is by hypotheses testing. This technique is not always straightforward, and it is worthwhile to explain how it works.

When a researcher suspects that a certain fact is the case, for instance, that smoking is related to lung cancer, she formulates a hypothesis to test. The hypothesis being tested is the *negation* of the conjecture that we are trying to prove. Trying to be very careful, we state that something has been proven only if it is objectively beyond a reasonable doubt. Thus, we allow the negation of the conjecture the benefit of the doubt. In this example, the researcher would formulate as the null hypothesis, $H_0$, the claim that smoking *is not related* to lung cancer. The hypothesis that it is related will play the role of the alternative, often denoted $H_1$.

Next, the researcher selects a test, which is a procedure of taking a sample, performing some calculations, and based on these calculations, making the decision of rejecting $H_0$ or not. The sample will typically consist of i.i.d. random variables from the relevant populations, say, the population of smokers and the population of nonsmokers. Then the test could say that the null hypothesis should be rejected if and only if the percentage of lung cancer cases in the smokers' population is sufficiently higher than the percentage in the population of nonsmokers.

What is sufficiently high? We start by observing that statistical proofs almost never attain the degree of certainty of logical proofs. However large the samples, and however stark the difference between the two populations, it is still possible that the differences in the samples are due to coincidence. Realizing that this is the normal state of affairs, we can ask how much of a coincidence needs to be assumed to reconcile the data with the null hypothesis. That is, if we do give $H_0$ the benefit of the doubt and assume it is true, how likely would it be to observe that which we have indeed observed? If the answer is extremely unlikely, we end up rejecting $H_0$, thereby proving the alternative.

In other words, the basic logic of hypothesis testing is similar to showing that it is embarrassing or ridiculous to hold on to the negation of the claim we try to prove. For instance, a cigarette manufacturer insists that smoking has nothing to do with lung cancer. A priori, this would be a valid conjecture. But if we see that, in very large samples, almost all the smokers suffer from the disease and almost all nonsmokers do not, we will ask the manufacturer, "Well, what do you say now?" "Just a coincidence" might be the answer. Then we should ask, "OK, let's try to quantify it—how unlikely was the event that you wish us to believe has occurred by chance? Let's assume that the two phenomena are not related, and compute what would have been the (maximal) probability of observing the data we have actually observed under your assumption." Suppose we go through the calculation and find that this maximal probability is .001. Now we can turn back to the producer and say, "Sorry, we don't believe your conjecture. Everything is theoretically possible. But you ask us to believe that we have just witnessed a very unlikely event. It makes much more sense to admit that there is a relation between the two phenomena."

It is important to realize that hypotheses testing does not rely on an a priori judgment of the likelihood of the hypothesis being correct (versus its negation). Such a priori judgments are bound to be subjective. Hypotheses testing aspires to objectivity. Hence it cannot rely on subjective prior beliefs, reflecting bias, prejudice, or preconception.

There are some important caveats regarding the interpretation of hypotheses tests:

• When a hypothesis is not rejected based on the data, it need not be correct or even strongly supported by the data. A failure to reject a hypothesis (sometimes referred to as *acceptance*) only means that it could not be rejected. To prove the hypothesis $H_0$ we would need to switch roles, define $H_0$ as the alternative, and attempt to reject the negation of $H_0$. Often, neither the hypothesis nor its negation can be rejected based on the data available. Importantly, when one restricts oneself to objective statements, one has to remain silent on many issues.

• While hypotheses testing attempts to be objective, there are always sources of subjectivity. In many real life situations, there is more than one way of formulating a hypothesis. For a particular hypothesis there are many possible tests. And the degree of coincidence allowed, called the significance level, can also be chosen at various levels.

Scientific studies try to cope with these sources of subjectivity in various ways. For example, a particular conjecture about real life events can be tested in the guise of different formal hypotheses. For many simple hypotheses there are standard tests that are selected by theoretical considerations, so that there is less leeway in choosing the test according to one's goals. And there are standards of the significance level that have become the norms in a given scientific community. Having said that, it is useful to recall that objectivity is always qualified.

• An effect that is statistically significant need not be significant in any intuitive sense of the word. Suppose, for example, that the probability of developing lung cancer for nonsmokers is .0129 and for smokers .0131. In this case, for large enough sample sizes, we can be confident that we will eventually reject the hypothesis that the probability in the two populations is identical (or lower for smokers), thereby proving that smoking is related to lung cancer. Further, this will be true for any level of significance chosen as a threshold. But the difference is not very important; smoking results in a less than 2 percent increase in probability (relative to the base of 1.29 percent), and the overall danger is anyhow rather low. In fact, given these (hypothetical) numbers, a smoker might find it rational to keep smoking even though the probability of the disease is significantly higher for smokers than for non-smokers (in the statistical sense of *significance*).

Statistics has developed more refined techniques to cope with this problem. In particular, the concept of effect size attempts to trade off the size of the effect with the size of the sample that was used to prove its significance. But such refined concepts are rarely reported in the popular press. In fact, when we read that "scientists have shown that..." we typically know very little about the details of the tests that were employed.

• Another problem is that significance levels are computed when one plans the study a priori. In actual studies, one often comes up with conjectures after the data have been gathered. In fact, this practice is crucial for scientific discovery. It is only natural to keep developing theories while observing the data. But the notion of significance assumes this is not the case. Moreover, if one measures many variables in a given population, one is likely to be able to find *some* hypotheses that can be rejected post hoc. Scientific empirical studies are rather careful in trying to avoid this phenomenon. But, again, our everyday consumption of scientific findings is often susceptible to such pitfalls.

# III  Group Choices

We have so far assumed a single decision maker. This decision maker can be a person or an organization, such as a state or a firm. It can also be an animal or a species or even an inanimate object such as a robot. All these decision makers can be ascribed a utility function and can be viewed as making decisions under certainty or uncertainty, according to objective or subjective beliefs, which reflect correct or erroneous statistical inference. In short, the discussion thus far can be quite general in terms of its applications. But it says nothing about what choices should be, or would be made, in case there is more than one decision maker involved.

Many of the problems in the social sciences involve more than one individual, and one main question they deal with is how to reconcile different individuals' preferences. We may think of economic markets, where an alternative specifies how much of each good will be allocated to each individual. In this example the individuals may be similar to each other, but because each consumes her share of the goods, and each prefers more rather than less, they are likely to have conflicts of interest. We may also think of a country's foreign policy, where all citizens experience the same outcome but value it differently. And there are situations in which an alternative specifies each individual's private consumption as well as the economy's joint consumption of public goods (such as schools, hospitals, roads, military). In this case disagreements may arise partly because of the allocation of private goods and partly because of differences in tastes.

Each individual $i$ has preferences over alternatives. Assume they are represented by the maximization of a utility function $u_i$. Can we define society's preference given the individual preferences? In other words, can we aggregate preferences?

The discussion of individual choice did not draw a very clear distinction between descriptive and normative theories. The reason is that our notion of rationality is closely related to that of a successful normative theory, and both have to do with a comparison between theory and behavior. A normative theory is successful if people can be convinced that they would like to follow it. A theory describes rational choice if people are not embarrassed to find out that it applies to them, or if people cannot be convinced that they would not like to follow it. The two concepts are not identical because it is possible that I can convince you neither that a certain mode of behavior is wrong for you (hence, it is rational for you) nor that it is right for you (hence, it is not effective as a normative theory). Yet, these concepts are close.

This is not the case when we discuss groups of individuals. It is possible that each decision maker is rational and cannot be convinced to change his behavior unilaterally but that the group can be convinced to change its behavior jointly. For example, we may consider a legal system and provide a theory of rational choices of individuals given the system, whereas we can also consider a normative theory that suggests changing the legal system. Thus, discussing rational choices in groups, we need to draw a sharper distinction between a descriptive theory, describing rational choices by individuals, and a normative theory, recommending modes of behavior to society as a whole.

This part begins with a normative approach, focusing on how preferences should be aggregated. The discussion leads to the notion of Pareto optimality. This rather weak criterion serves as the benchmark for the descriptive discussion that follows.

# 6    Aggregation of Preferences

## 6.1  Summation of Utilities

It appears that the simplest way of aggregating preferences is to add up the utility functions of all individuals involved and to maximize this sum. If we take the utility function $u_i$ as a measure of the well-being of individual $i$, the sum of utilities across individuals will give us a measure of the overall well-being in society. Maximizing this sum appears to be the right thing to do.

This maximization is often referred to as utilitarianism. This term was coined in the late eighteenth century by Jeremy Bentham, who suggested that one should bring about "the greatest happiness of the greatest number." John Stuart Mill in the mid-nineteenth century also contributed to and refined this philosophical position. In particular, he argued that there are determinants of utility that should not be endorsed by the utilitarian aggregation. For example, Schadenfreude (enjoying someone else's misfortune) is commonly viewed as a type of enjoyment that should be excluded from the summation of utilities to be maximized by society.

Utilitarianism is often criticized because it derives the notions of good and evil from consequences rather than from general principles. Immanuel Kant, the most prominent anti-utilitarianist, argued that morality of an act should be determined by the general rules one should follow rather than by the specific outcomes it may lead to. In terms of formal models, this critique may be rephrased as saying that the consequences we consider should also specify which rules have been followed and which have been violated. Such a reinterpretation of consequences may allow the formal model of utilitarianism to capture certain nonutilitarian ideas. That is, one can use utilitarianism as a paradigm rather than as a theory (see section 7.1.8).

The addition of utility functions across individuals is reminiscent of the notion of expected utility, in which we add up utility functions across different states of the world or different possible scenarios. In fact, this mathematical analogy is quite deep. John Harsanyi (in the 1950s) and John Rawls (in the 1970s) suggested that when considering a social choice problem, one should ask what the choice would have been if the decision maker had not been born yet and his identity was not known.[1] In this "original position" behind a "veil of ignorance," the social choice problem is actually a problem of decision under uncertainty. If one is willing to accept this mental leap backward in time, and if one maximizes expected utility when facing uncertainty, one may find this a reason to support utilitarianism in a social choice problem.

One may be willing to discuss the hypothetical decision problem behind the veil of ignorance but reject the principle of maximization of expected utility in this problem. Different criteria for decision under uncertainty would result in different approaches to the social choice problem. Indeed, Rawls suggested that the more conservative criterion of maximizing the worst possible outcome (maxmin) results in a preference for the social policy that maximizes the well-being of the individual who is worst off.

There are several problems with the attempt to operationalize utilitarianism by summing utility functions. First, it is not obvious that the utility functions used to represent preferences actually measure well-being or happiness (see chapter 10). Second, the utility function that describes an individual's choices is not unique. Even the vNM utility function for choice under risk is only given up to a shift (addition of a constant) and multiplication by a positive constant. This freedom is sufficient to make utilitarianism ill-defined.

To see this, suppose there are two individuals, 1 and 2. For each alternative $x$, $u_1(x)$ is the utility of individual 1, and $u_2(x)$ is the utility of individual 2. The choice of a transformation is immaterial if we only want to find the best alternative for a single individual. Maximizing $u_1(x)$ and maximizing $2u_1(x) + 3$ are equivalent. Even the maximization of the expectation of $u_1(x)$ is equivalent to the maximization of the expectation of $2u_1(x) + 3$. Moreover, adding 3 to $u_1$ will not make a difference even for the maximization of the sum of the utilities. If we do so, every social alternative $x$ will be evaluated by three more aggregate utility points, but the selection of the best alternative $x$ will not be affected by this shift. However, multiplication by the number 2 will make a big difference; it determines individual 1's weight in society.

For concreteness, let $U$ be the utilitarian aggregation function with the original functions,

$$U(x) = u_1(x) + u_2(x),$$

and let $V$ be the corresponding aggregation after the modification of individual 1's utility

$$V(x) = 2u_1(x) + 3 + u_2(x).$$

Suppose there are two alternatives, $x$ and $y$, with the following utility values for the two individuals:

|   | $u_1$ | $u_2$ |
|---|---|---|
| $x$ | 0 | 10 |
| $y$ | 8 | 0 |

Clearly,

$$U(x) > U(y) \quad \text{but} \quad V(x) < V(y).$$

In other words, the maximizing the sum of utilities would give us different societal preferences if we choose $u_1$ or $(2u_1 + 3)$ to represent individual 1's preferences, even though the two functions are equivalent in terms of their observable meaning. Whether $u_1$ or $(2u_1 + 3)$ is individual 1's "true" utility function is devoid of scientific content. Yet, the preference between $x$ and $y$ depends on this question (among others).

Another problem with the maximization of utility values has to do with truthful reports. Suppose we have a preference questionnaire that could measure individuals' utility functions. Knowing that the measurement will be used for the addition of utilities across individuals, each individual has an incentive to report values that are spread over a larger scale, so as to effectively get a higher weight in the social summation. Thus, even if we had a way to tell the difference between a function $u_1$ and $(2u_1 + 3)$, we should not assume that all individuals truthfully report their utility functions.

Both problems—the nonuniqueness of the utility function and the manipulation of individual reports—can be solved if one ignores the actual utility functions of the individuals and applies utilitarianism to a common utility function that is imposed on these individuals by the social planner. This social planner, or impartial observer, judges the utility of outcomes (such as bundles of goods in an economy) and then, neither resorting to questionnaires nor paying attention to individual preferences, chooses an alternative that maximizes the sum of this (single) utility function across individuals.

This idea has great merit, and it is probably a rather good model of what we do in practice. Suppose there are two individuals, 1, who has an income of $100 per day, and 2, who has an income of $5 per day. A redistribution of income is being considered. Suppose individual 1 argues that increasing her income from $100 to $101 per day will result in a huge increase in utility, much greater than the loss of one dollar for individual 2, who might go down from $5 to $4 a day. Such an argument would seem preposterous. But if we have no way to make *interpersonal comparisons of utility*, it is not obvious how we can rule it out. By contrast, if we adopt a single utility function, apply it to all individuals' incomes, and sum it up, such an argument will be irrelevant. And for a reasonable utility function we will find that the loss of utility in going down from $5 to $4 per day is greater than the gain derived from going up from $100 to $101 per day.

Indeed, if we believe that the marginal utility of money is decreasing (with respect to the amount of money we already have), that is, if we assume that the utility function is concave, summation of this utility across individuals will prefer egalitarian allocations. This is precisely the same logic as for risk aversion; a concave utility results in a higher sum when its argument is smoothed across the summands. If we sum over states of the world (in the case of expected utility), we prefer less risk; if we sum over individuals (in the case of utilitarianism), we prefer less inequality.

This is one justification for progressive taxation, namely, the policy that the rich pay a higher marginal tax than the poor. Having to make decisions, we are forced to choose between giving one more dollar to the rich or to the poor, and we prefer the latter.

Note, however, that attributing a prespecified utility function to all individuals, irrespective of their personal tastes, does not amount to interpersonal comparisons of utility. It is in fact a way to avoid the question by ignoring individuals' utility functions. This approach makes sense for the distribution of income, but it doesn't seem very satisfactory when we consider more general alternatives, with more than one good. People do differ in their tastes, and this is part of the reason for trade. Also, many choice problems are not about redistribution of goods but about choices that the group makes as a whole. When a group of friends debates which movie to go to, and when a country decides whether to wage war on another country, there are differences in preferences and in opinions about what is in the best interest of the group. In these situations, we do not have a function $u$ that describes the preferences of each individual in the group.

To conclude, the aggregation of utilities is an appealing option that has many conceptual and practical difficulties. It seems applicable mostly for redistribution problems in which differences in tastes may be ignored. More generally, we understand why economists, for the most part, prefer to avoid interpersonal comparisons of utility.

## 6.2 Condorcet's Paradox

A major conceptual problem with the summation of utilities in the previous discussion was that an individual's utility function is given only up to monotone transformations. That is, it is *ordinal*, not *cardinal*. It therefore makes sense to restrict attention to observable data, namely, to the pairwise comparisons made by each individual, and see what can be said about them. In particular, when we compare two alternatives, the most natural thing to do is to have a vote and follow the majority. This appears the most democratic and also most common nonviolent way to resolve conflicts or to aggregate preferences.

Unfortunately, such a resolution of conflicts is hardly rational. In the eighteenth century the Marquis de Condorcet presented the following paradox. Assume there are three alternatives, $x$, $y$, $z$, and three individuals who have the following preferences:

|        | Individual |     |     |
|--------|------------|-----|-----|
|        | 1          | 2   | 3   |
| Rank 1 | $x$        | $z$ | $y$ |
| Rank 2 | $y$        | $x$ | $z$ |
| Rank 3 | $z$        | $y$ | $x$ |

where each column specifies the preferences of one individual, with alternatives ranked from top to bottom. When we put $x$ and $y$ to a majority vote, $x$ wins two-thirds of the votes; individuals 1 and 2 prefer

$x$ to $y$, and only individual 3 prefers $y$ to $x$. Next, if we ask the individuals to vote between $x$ and $z$, $z$ wins two-thirds of the votes (individuals 2 and 3). Finally, when this recent winner, $z$, is confronted with $y$, the latter wins, again by a two-thirds majority (individuals 1 and 3). Majority vote may generate cycles. Since it fails to guarantee transitivity of preferences, this method cannot be relied upon to aggregate preferences.

Condorcet's paradox also indicates how sequential votes can be manipulated. Suppose I am chairing a meeting in which one of the alternatives $x$, $y$, $z$ will be chosen. Also, one of the alternatives is the status quo and will be the default decision if no decision is made. (Generally, if there is an option of not deciding, we expect it to be listed as one of the alternatives.) Suppose that I know the preferences of the people at the meeting and that they are split into three equal-size groups, having the preferences of 1, 2, and 3 in the preceding table. I actually prefer $x$. I may start by suggesting that we first decide between $y$ and $z$. There is a majority for $y$, and $z$ is ruled out. Now I suggest that we vote on the choice between $y$ and $x$. There is a majority for $x$, and I suggest we record this as our democratic vote. Everyone might know that $z$ could beat $x$, but it would seem counterproductive to raise the issue again; after all, $z$ has already been voted out, hasn't it?

Clearly, this applies not only to $x$ but to any other alternative that is a preferred choice. This may suggest that the person controlling the agenda will fully control the outcome of the election. In reality one may expect people to be sophisticated enough to see where the process is going, to challenge the order of issues on the agenda, and maybe also to vote strategically, that is, to vote in a way that need not correspond to their true preferences. But the main point remains. Majority votes between pairs of alternatives are a great idea if there are only two alternatives. Beyond that, they are problematic.

## 6.3   Impossibility Theorems

### 6.3.1   Arrow's Theorem
One might wonder what it is about majority votes that may result in intransitivities. It may be hard to imagine more sensible ways to aggregate binary preferences, but perhaps we would be able to find a method of aggregation that would not be prone to such incoherent choices. Unfortunately, this is not the case, as Kenneth Arrow has

proved.[2] Thinking about new aggregation methods will not help because none exist.

Here I describe Arrow's theorem informally. (A formal statement is given in appendix B.) Assume there are at least three alternatives. Each individual has a transitive preference relation over these alternatives. The input to the social choice problem is a profile, that is, a list of preferences, one for each individual. We consider functions that accept as input such profiles of preferences and yield as output another preference relation, that of society. We wish society's preferences to be transitive (as are the preferences of each individual). Assume that all ranking involved (individuals' and society's) allow no indifferences (ties). This assumption is not crucial, but it slightly simplifies the statement of one condition.

Arrow formulated two axioms on the aggregation function.

**Unanimity**  If everyone prefers $x$ to $y$, then so should society. It is generally taken to be a minimal condition that any notion of aggregation should satisfy. Indeed, to think of a counterexample, one would need to imagine a situation in which everyone prefers $x$ to $y$ but the social planner decides to choose $y$ over $x$. It is not clear on what grounds such a choice could be justified.

**Independence of Irrelevant Alternatives (IIA)**  The social preference between two specific alternatives, $x$ and $y$, only depends on individual preferences between these two alternatives. Whereas unanimity is an axiom that applies to a given profile of preferences, the IIA is an axiom of coherence; it requires that the aggregation of preferences in different profiles be related to each other in a way that (presumably) makes sense. Note that if one has a particular profile of individual preferences, the IIA axiom does not restrict social preferences in any way. It only says that *if*, given one profile, society prefers $x$ to $y$, *then*, given other profiles (in which every individual has the same preferences between $x$ and $y$ as in the first profile), society should also prefer $x$ to $y$. This axiom is discussed in detail later. At this point it's sufficient to understand its basic logic.

Arrow's result is that the only functions that satisfy the two conditions are *dictatorial*, that is, functions that always adopt the preferences of a particular individual. It is easy to see that such functions will do the trick. If society's preferences are always defined to be the preferences of individual 1, for example, then (unanimity) when everyone prefers $x$ to $y$, in particular, individual 1 prefers $x$ to $y$, so will society; and (IIA) society's preference between any two $x$ and $y$ depends only on the way these two alternatives are ranked by the individuals; in fact, it depends only the ranking of these alternatives by one of these individuals.

Thus, with $n$ individuals, there are $n$ different dictatorial functions that satisfy both of Arrow's conditions. The amazing result is that these are the only ones.

It is important to understand that the object of the impossibility theorem is a *function*. That is, we seek a general rule of aggregation of preferences, which should be prepared to aggregate *any* profile of preferences. Arrow's impossibility theorem does not say that in a particular society, that is, for a particular profile of preferences, there is no way to aggregate preferences. It says that there is no way to do it for *all* possible profiles in a coherent way.

This result is called Arrow's impossibility theorem. It refers to as *impossibility* because, whatever aggregation of preferences should mean, it cannot mean having a dictator. If $f$ is dictatorial, it doesn't perform any aggregation—no compromises, no give-and-take, nothing that has a flavor of democracy. Or, differently put, the theorem says that any aggregation that is nontrivial (in the sense that it is nondictatorial) and that satisfies the two axioms will not produce a transitive order. If we use such a method of aggregation, the social preferences will exhibit some intransitivities, as in Condorcet's paradox.

### 6.3.2 Scoring Rules and Grading Systems

While the IIA axiom appears very natural, it is hardly as compelling as the unanimity axiom. Consider, for instance, the following two profiles, with alternatives ranked from top (most preferred) to bottom (least preferred):

|        | Individual | | | |
|--------|---|---|---|---|
|        | 1 | 2 | 3 | 4 |
| Rank 1 | $x$ | $x$ | $a$ | $a$ |
| Rank 2 | $a$ | $a$ | $b$ | $b$ |
| Rank 3 | $b$ | $b$ | $y$ | $y$ |
| Rank 4 | $y$ | $y$ | $x$ | $x$ |

and

|        | Individual |     |     |     |
|--------|------------|-----|-----|-----|
|        | 1          | 2   | 3   | 4   |
| Rank 1 | $a$        | $a$ | $y$ | $y$ |
| Rank 2 | $b$        | $b$ | $a$ | $a$ |
| Rank 3 | $x$        | $x$ | $b$ | $b$ |
| Rank 4 | $y$        | $y$ | $x$ | $x$ |

In both profiles the relative ranking of $x$ and $y$ are the same. The first two individuals prefer $x$ to $y$, and the second two individuals exhibit the opposite preference. Hence, the IIA axiom requires that the social aggregation function rank $x$ over $y$ in both profiles, or $y$ over $x$ in both. But this doesn't seem quite right. In the first profile, the two individuals who prefer $x$ to $y$ place the former at the very top and the latter at the very bottom, whereas the two individuals who prefer $y$ to $x$ rank both at the bottom. It appears that those who prefer $x$ to $y$ feel more strongly about their preference than those who prefer $y$ to $x$. One could say there is a reason to prefer $x$ over $y$ in this case. In the second profile the situation is reversed. This time the same reasoning would lead to preferring $y$ over $x$. This would be a violation of the IIA axiom.

But what is meant by those who prefer $x$ to $y$ "feel more strongly" than those who have the opposite preference? We know we can't compare preferences across individuals. Yet, the existence of other alternatives and the way they are ranked relative to $x$ and $y$—in between the pair $x$, $y$ or outside it—may be informative. Importantly, the number of alternatives that are between $x$ and $y$ is an observable quantity that may be used as an indirect measure of strength of preference. Indeed, if each alternative is assigned a value from a given distribution in an i.i.d. manner, then the number of alternatives that happen to get values between the values of $x$ and $y$ will tell us something about the difference between these values.

In short, the IIA axiom may not be as compelling as it first appears. And if we are willing to drop this axiom, there are many ways to aggregate preferences so as to satisfy the unanimity axiom and obtain transitive social preferences without appointing a dictator. For example, suppose that each individual fills in a grade sheet where the grade of an alternative is its position in the rank from the bottom. In the first profile in this section, the grade of $x$ will be 4 for the first two individuals, and 1 for the next two. The grades of $y$ will be 1, 1, 2, 2. It is natural to add up these grades to define a social utility function (or equivalently, to compute their average). We then find that $x$ has an overall grade higher than $y$'s in the first profile and that this is reversed in the second profile.

This grading system is known as the Borda count; it was suggested by Jean-Charles de Borda in 1770. Clearly, this aggregation function satisfies unanimity. It is, however, not a unique grading system that satisfies unanimity because one need not assign grades that are equally spaced. For instance, with four alternatives one can decide that, for each individual, the grades of the alternatives are 0, 1, 9, 10. Again, if all individuals prefer $x$ to $y$, each individual will allocate to $x$ a higher grade than to $y$, and consequently $x$ will have a higher sum than will $y$.

Grading systems in which the grade is determined by the alternative's rank are also known as scoring rules. More generally, we can think of grading systems that allow ties, the possibility that different individuals use different scales, and so forth. The key feature is that a ballot cast by an individual assigns a numerical grade to each alternative, and alternatives are ranked according to the sum of their grades. All these systems have the nice feature that if one takes the union of two disjoint populations in each of which $x$ is preferred to $y$, this preference will be also exhibited by the union of the two populations.[3]

In a plurality vote each individual chooses one alternative, and society's ranking is defined by the number of votes each alternative receives. This is a special case of a scoring rule in which the scores (grades) are restricted to be in 0 or 1, and moreover each voter can assign 1 only to one alternative.

Another special case retains the restriction to scores in 0 or 1 but allows each voter to assign 1 to any number of alternatives. When we sum up the scores, we basically count, for each alternative, how many individuals assigned it 1. This voting method is called *approval voting*; it was suggested in the 1970s by Robert Weber and by Steven Brams and Peter Fishburn.[4] The idea is that voters are not asked to choose one candidate but to say who are the candidates of whom they approve.

To see the advantage of approval voting over a plurality vote, consider the following example. In the U.S. presidential elections, there are two main contenders, representing the Democratic and Republican parties. There are often also independent candidates, who almost never stand a serious chance of winning, but they do run for various reasons. For example, a Green candidate, promoting the environment as a single issue, may not win the election, but he does make an important point and can change the course of the election. It has been argued that such a candidate should drop out because he pulls notes away from the Democratic candidate, who is generally closer to him in his views.

It is not hard to see how this can happen in a variety of examples. There is always a danger of splitting a camp into smaller subcamps and thereby losing the majority to a party that is in fact a minority party. For example, assume that a left-wing party has 60 percent of the votes and can defeat the right-wing party, which has only 40 percent of the votes. Then the left-wing party is split into two smaller parties, with votes of 30 percent each, whose positions differ only in minor details. Together they stand, divided they fall. Clearly, the right-wing party will win the election, having the largest share of the votes. Still, a majority of the voters prefer either one of the other parties to the winner.

One possible solution, which is implemented in the French presidential elections, is to have two voting rounds; in the second, only the top two candidates compete. Thus, in the previous example, in the second round one of the left-wing parties would defeat the right-wing one. But sometimes two rounds will not suffice. By contrast, approval voting seems to alleviate this problem. For instance, if a left-wing party splits into two, voters may cast a ballot that approves of both of them without weakening them as a block.

### 6.3.3 Gibbard-Satterthwaite's Theorem

Despite the optimistic tone of the last section, the problem is not actually solved by approval voting or by scoring rules in general. The reason is that voters might still have an incentive to report preferences that do not accurately reflect their opinion. In the previous example, suppose there are two left-wing parties, supported by 60 percent of the voters, and a single right-wing party, supported by 40 percent of the voters. Approval voting has been chosen as the voting rule, and I'm a left-wing voter. How should I vote?

I may cast a ballot that approves of the two left-wing parties. But if all left-wing voters do so, each of these parties will have 60 percent approval, and both will beat the right-wing party. This is good news for me. I am more relaxed knowing that a left-wing party will be elected.

But I may still care about which one it is. If I have some minor preference for one over the other, it may make more sense for me to approve
*only* my most preferred party, thus giving it an edge in the competition
for the most widely approved party. But if everyone votes this way, we
are back to a plurality vote, and the two left-wing parties will lose the
election.

Thus, approval voting, like a plurality vote, encourages strategic
thinking. Voters may have an incentive not to vote as if they were dic-
tators but to take into account what they believe other voters will do
and respond optimally to that. This notion of strategic voting, which
is contrasted with sincere voting, need not carry negative connotations.
A voter who prefers to support the Democratic candidate even if
her top choice is the independent Green candidate is not dishonest
in any way. Such a voter recognizes that she lives in a democratic society, where the result of the election is going to be some compromise
among different voters' preferences. Trying to support the preferred
candidate among those who have a chance to win can be viewed as an
instance of separating the feasible from the desirable. We could call
this phenomenon sophisticated voting and distinguish it from naive
voting.

But even if we do not frown upon strategic voting as an immoral
phenomenon, we may be concerned that it might bring about un-
desired outcomes. For example, suppose that for some reason everyone believes that the independent candidate is going to get more votes
than the Democratic one. If this is the prevailing belief, the majority of
the Democrats, who actually prefer their candidate to the independent
candidate, may end up voting for the latter rather than the former, for
the same type of reasoning. In other words, strategic voting allows various outcomes, some of which may not reflect the majority of the voters' preferences.

It is therefore natural to ask whether we can have a voting system in
which voters can always report their actual preferences? That is, can
we construct a mechanism whereby voters report preferences, candidates are ranked as a function of these reported preferences, and no
voter will ever have an incentive to misrepresent her preferences?

A negative answer was given by Allan Gibbard and Mark Satterthwaite (in the 1970s).[5] They showed that the only methods of voting in which such incentives do not exist are dictatorial, namely,
mechanisms that pick a particular individual and follow her reported
preferences.

### 6.3.4   An Argument for Approval Voting

In approval voting, voters are not asked to report their entire ranking of the alternatives but only a subset of alternatives, which can be interpreted as acceptable or sufficiently desirable. In this system voters never have an incentive to approve of an alternative $y$ that is worst in their eyes, and they always have an incentive to approve of an alternative $x$ that is best in their eyes. If only three alternatives exist, this means that voters will never have an incentive to approve of an alternative they like less than some other alternative they decided not to approve of. Specifically, if a voter prefers $x$ to $y$ to $z$, the voter might approve of $x$ alone, or of $x$ and $y$, but he will never wish to vote for, say, $y$ alone, or for $z$ but not for $y$, and so on.

This property is called *sincere voting* because the voter does not "lie" by approving of $y$ but not of $x$ while in fact preferring $x$ to $y$. Unfortunately, approval voting is not guaranteed to give rise to sincere voting when there are more than three alternatives.

### 6.3.5   Conclusion

The notion of aggregation of different individuals' preferences is fraught with difficulties. Some pertain to the definition of utility, some to the coherence of aggregation, and some to the incentives to report preferences truthfully. When we consider the workings of actual democracies and deplore the process of political compromise, it is useful to keep in mind that even theoretically we don't have magic solutions.

### 6.4   Pareto Optimality/Efficiency

In light of the difficulties with aggregation of preferences, one may take a much more humble point of view. Instead of saying what we wish to do, we can at least rule out some things we are quite sure we don't want to do. In particular, we should respect unanimity. It seems unobjectionable that if every individual finds $x$ at least as good as $y$, so should society. Moreover, if every individual finds $x$ at least as good as $y$, and for at least one individual $x$ is strictly better than $y$, we may feel that $x$ should be strictly preferred to $y$ by society.

This relation is called *Pareto dominance*. Intuitively, $x$ Pareto-dominates $y$ if, when $x$ and $y$ are put to a vote, there would be some individuals who vote for $x$ and some that are indifferent, but no one would object to choosing $x$ over $y$.

An alternative $x$ is called *Pareto-optimal* or *Pareto-efficient* if it is not Pareto-dominated by any other feasible alternative $z$. The terms *Pareto-optimal* and *Pareto-efficient* are synonymous, and they are both very popular. Unfortunately, both are misleading. This is a sorry state of affairs in light of the fact that the concept is one of the most important in economics, game theory, and social choice theory. Often, people read too much into the term *optimal* and too little into *efficient*. Section 6.5.2 discusses, among the limitations of the concept, why *optimal* means less than it may suggest. Here I explain why *efficient* deserves more than it connotes.

To understand the term *efficiency*, it is useful to think of an economy with individuals who consume private goods. The term is more general and can apply to any social choice problem, such as the choice of a country's foreign policy, but *efficiency* probably originates with production. Indeed, Pareto efficiency generalizes the requirement that resources be used efficiently. Suppose that production is not efficient and that we could use the same resources and let each individual have more of each good. Assuming that individuals like the goods, this implies that the alternative we started out with was not Pareto-efficient. Thus, technological inefficiency implies Pareto inefficiency. Equivalently, Pareto efficiency requires efficient production.

But efficient production is not sufficient for Pareto efficiency. Suppose, for example, that we produce, very efficiently, huge amounts of broccoli. There is no way to improve upon the process and get more broccoli with the same resources. Alas, no one in the economy likes broccoli. Some people like bananas, and some people like mangos. Instead of all this broccoli, we could have produced some bananas, which would have made the banana eaters happier, or some mangos, which the mango eaters would have appreciated. In this case production is efficient, but the allocation is not Pareto-efficient. We could have made everyone better off, not by producing more of the disliked good but by producing a different good that fits individuals' tastes.

Next, suppose we produce the right products and do this efficiently. We do not waste land and water on broccoli but produce instead bananas and mangos. Moreover, production is efficient, and we can't grow more bananas or mangos than we currently do. But one little problem remains: it so happens that the mangos are in the hands of the banana eaters, and vice versa. Again, the economy is technologically efficient and even produces the right goods in the aggregate. But it does not allocate the goods efficiently. We could obtain a Pareto improvement if individuals were to trade, exchanging bananas for mangos, so that everyone has more of what they like.

Thus, in the context of an economy, Pareto efficiency requires that the goods be produced efficiently, that the right quantities of products be produced, and that they be allocated wisely. Often people take the word *efficient* to refer only to technological efficiency, with connotations of machines, mass production, long shifts, and so forth. All these may indeed be related to Pareto efficiency, but this concept also takes into account individuals and their needs and desires. In particular, working more hours a day will result in more product, but if workers prefer to have more leisure, this will not be a Pareto improvement.

Finally, recall that the concept is not restricted to economies with goods and production. It applies to any social choice problem, and it only means that we can't make some individuals better off without hurting others.

It appears reasonable to restrict attention to Pareto-efficient alternatives. Choosing anything else, say an alternative $y$ that is not Pareto-efficient, means that we could have chosen an $x$ that is better than $y$ according to some and at least as good as $y$ according to all, yet we picked $y$. Pareto optimality/efficiency is therefore a minimal condition on the aggregation of preferences. This condition does not try to get into the truly difficult trade-offs, where there is real conflict, when one has to make interpersonal comparisons of utility. Many economists believe that the role of science—economics as well as other social sciences—ends with the notion of Pareto optimality, and that any further choices, which do involve real trade-offs, should be left to others (philosophers, politicians). Other economists are willing to delve into the theoretically less secure grounds of non-unanimous preferences. The desirability of Pareto optimality, however, enjoys a wide consensus. Unfortunately, even this mild criterion is not always easy to satisfy.

## 6.5   Limitations of Pareto Optimality

Much of the discussion that follows, as well as many discussions in economics and game theory, revolves around Pareto optimality. Moreover, economic discussions in the popular press often refer to optimality or efficiency. Many readers are not aware that these terms mean

Pareto efficiency, and they often do not know what this means. It is therefore important to understand the term and to be aware of some of its limitations.

### 6.5.1   Silent on Equality

Because the notion of Pareto optimality (or efficiency) veers away from interpersonal comparisons of utility, it says nothing about equality. Assume there is one loaf of bread to share between two individuals, that each individual cares only about how much she gets, and that she prefers more to less. Under these assumptions, *any* split will be Pareto-optimal. One individual can have the entire loaf while the other one would be starving to death, and this allocation will be Pareto-optimal.

### 6.5.2   A Partial Order

The Pareto dominance relation is a partial order, that is, it does not compare any pair of alternatives. The truly interesting questions, where some individuals (strictly) prefer one alternative and others prefer different alternatives, are not resolved by Pareto domination.

As a result, the term *optimality* may be confusing. By definition, an alternative $x$ is *optimal* if no alternative $y$ is strictly better than $x$. An alternative $x$ is an *optimum* if $x$ is at least as good as any other alternative.

When the relation "at least as good as" is complete, and any pair of alternatives can be compared, it is true that an optimal alternative is an optimum. An alternative that cannot be improved upon is also a best alternative. It may not be a unique best alternative, but it is among the best, and all best alternatives are equivalent.

This is not the case when we discuss partial orders. When an order is partial, an optimum has to be optimal, but the converse is not true. An optimal alternative need not be at least as good as all the others. It may well be incomparable to some. To consider an extreme case, if no alternative can be compared to any other, all alternatives are optimal but none is an optimum.

It is important to stress this fact because the term *optimal* tends to confuse people. We tend to think in terms of complete orders, such as "taller than," "bigger than," "faster than," and so forth. Much of our intuition is therefore based on complete orders. With a complete order, it is true that an optimal alternative is at least as good as an alternative that is not optimal. But this is not the case with partial orders. For example, it may be the case that an alternative $x$ is Pareto-optimal, and $y$ is not Pareto-optimal, but $x$ does not Pareto-dominate $y$.

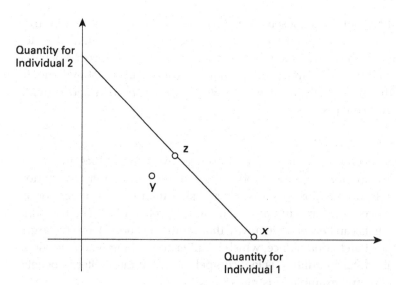

**Figure 6.1**

To consider a trivial example, assume there is one loaf of bread and two individuals. Let pairs of numbers denote possible amounts of bread given to the two individuals. For instance, $x = (1,0)$ is an alternative in which individual 1 gets the entire loaf and individual 2 gets nothing. An equal split of the entire loaf is given by $z = (0.5, 0.5)$, whereas $y = (0.4, 0.4)$ is an equal split that involves some waste (see figure 6.1).

Clearly, $x$ is Pareto-optimal because one cannot give both individuals more bread. By contrast, $y$ is not Pareto-optimal. In fact, $z$ Pareto-dominates $y$; both individuals have more bread in $z$ than in $y$. Yet, $x$ does not Pareto-dominate $y$; Individual 1 prefers $x$ to $y$, but individual 2 has the opposite preferences. Knowing that $y$ is not Pareto-optimal says that there *exists* an alternative that Pareto-dominates it. It need not be $x$.

Thus a Pareto-optimal alternative ($x$) need not Pareto-dominate a Pareto-suboptimal alternative ($y$). We should not automatically prefer any alternative that is Pareto-optimal to any other that isn't.

Examples of this type are often encountered in economics. It is possible that the market brings us to the point $x$ and that we care about equality and wish to make a transfer from individual 1 to 2. If the transfer involves taxation, we typically find that we lose Pareto optimality. Thus, we may end up at a point such as $y$. This *does not mean* that there will be a consensus against this transfer. It will not be true that the original point, by virtue of being Pareto-optimal, Pareto-dominates the new point, which is not Pareto-optimal. A social planner may well prefer a Pareto nonoptimal point to a Pareto-optimal one. In fact, this is typically what we do when we tax the rich and provide welfare to the poor.

### 6.5.3  Subjective Beliefs

When uncertainty is present, and no objective probabilities are given, people may use subjective probabilities. In these situations, the notion of Pareto domination has a weaker appeal than it does under conditions of certainty or with known, objective probabilities. The reason is that beliefs can be wrong in a way that utilities cannot. Hence the argument for Pareto dominance, which is rather compelling when individuals only differ in utilities, is less compelling when they differ in beliefs. The following example illustrates.[6]

Two gentlemen are about to engage in a duel. Each believes that he is going to kill the other and emerge unscathed with probability 90 percent. Each would rather flee town if he thought that the probability of his victory were 80 percent or lower. However, given their very different beliefs and their very different tastes (each prefers to be the one who survives the duel), they both prefer that the duel take place than not. In other words, having a duel Pareto-dominates not having a duel. But it is not obvious that this instance of Pareto domination is a very compelling reason to endorse the duel. Because the two gentlemen's beliefs are very different, and there are no beliefs that can simultaneously justify the preferences of both, it is possible that we should shrug our shoulders in face of this "domination."

The gentlemen need not be shooting at each other; they may simply be betting on the price of oil a year hence. If they are risk-averse, there are no joint beliefs that justify the decision of each to engage in the bet. We may not know who is wrong in his subjective beliefs, but we do know that they can't both be right. In such cases, we may settle for alternatives that are Pareto-dominated.

# 7    Games and Equilibria

## 7.1    Prisoner's Dilemma

### 7.1.1    The Basic Story

The original story of prisoner's dilemma is well known but worth repeating. Two guys commit a crime. They are arrested by the police, who are quite sure they are guilty but cannot prove it without at least one of them confessing. The police offer them the following deal. Each one of them can confess and get some credit for it. If only one confesses, he becomes a state witness, and not only is he not punished, he gets a reward (sent on a vacation to the Bahamas, away from his ex-collaborator's friends). If both confess, they will be punished but will get reduced sentences for helping the police. If neither confesses, the police honestly admit there is no way to convict them, and they are set free. All this is stated clearly and fairly—no cheating or asymmetric information is involved. However, the two suspects are sent to their own cells to contemplate their options and make their decisions independently.

Each prisoner reasons as follows. "Suppose that the other guy confesses. Then I face a choice between confessing and getting a reduced sentence, or not confessing and spending a longer time in jail. I should then confess. If, however, the other guy keeps silent, I can be set free by keeping silent myself, but I can do even better by confessing—I'll get a free trip to the Bahamas. It follows that I should confess no matter what the other guy does."

Thus, both confess and are sent to jail. However, if they had both kept silent, they would both have been set free. The striking thing about this example is that each individual does what is obviously rational for himself, but the result is not rational for them as a group.

The outcome, of both getting a reduced sentence, is Pareto-dominated by the alternative of both being set free.

It is useful to think of the situation as a game. A *game* consists of a set of players, a set of strategies for each player, and a utility function for each player, defined on the combinations of strategies of all players. Importantly, the choices of all players may affect not only themselves but all other players as well.

In this case, we have two players, each with two possible strategies, $C$ and $D$, where $C$ stands for cooperate and $D$ for defect. The strategy $C$ means cooperate with the other player (not with the police), and it refers in general to being nice to the other player, to following the social contract. The strategy $D$ means defect from the social contract, or being selfish. In this example, $C$ would mean keeping silent and not incriminating his friend, and $D$ means incriminating his friend for personal gain.

The situation can be modeled by the following game:

**Game 1.   Prisoner's Dilemma**

|       | $C$      | $D$      |
| ----- | -------- | -------- |
| $C$   | $(3,3)$  | $(0,4)$  |
| $D$   | $(4,0)$  | $(1,1)$  |

In each entry, the first number denotes the payoff (or utility) of player I (the row player) and the second the payoff of player II (the column player). The actual numbers do not matter very much.

This is a good opportunity to introduce the concept of domination between strategies in a game. The concept is basic, and its applicability extends beyond the prisoner's dilemma.

### 7.1.2   Dominated Strategies

Considering player I's choice, we observe that $D$ promises a strictly higher payoff than $C$ *whatever* player II chooses. (That is, $4 > 3$ in the first column, and $1 > 0$ in the second column.) In this case we say that strategy $D$ *strictly dominates* strategy $C$. We distinguish between *strict domination* of strategy $s$ over $t$, which means that the payoffs associated with $s$ are always strictly larger than those of $t$, and *weak domination*, where $s$ is guaranteed to yield a payoff that is at least as high as $t$'s, but for some strategies of the opponent's, $s$ can be just as good as $t$, provided that sometimes it is strictly better. Weak domination is formally equivalent to Pareto domination. If one replaces "strategies of the others" by "individuals," it is the same definition.

Consider the variant of the prisoner's dilemma presented in game 2. All payoffs are the same, apart from player I's payoff for the pair of choices $(D, C)$. For player I in this game, strategy $D$ weakly dominates strategy $C$, but this domination is not strict; there exists at least one choice of player II (namely, $C$), for which playing $D$ (for player I) yields the same payoff as playing $C$.

**Game 2.  A Variant of Prisoner's Dilemma**

|   | C | D |
|---|---|---|
| C | $(3,3)$ | $(0,4)$ |
| D | $(3,0)$ | $(1,1)$ |

It is commonly believed that dominated strategies will not be played. When applied to strict domination, this prediction is very compelling. Consider strategy $D$ for player II in game 2. As in the original game (game 1), it strictly dominates strategy $C$ (for player II). If we had only one row (for player I), the prediction that player II will play $D$ rather than $C$ would be tautological. This is how we assign utility numbers to alternatives, namely, in such a way that represents preferences. By contrast, the representation of preferences does not say anything about the choice in a decision matrix like the one shown for the game. Yet, it seems a rather mild assumption of rationality to argue that strictly dominating strategies should be selected over dominated ones, whether we take a descriptive or a normative approach. If the player is Bayesian and entertains probabilistic beliefs over the choices of the other player (namely, which row will be played), the vNM axioms also imply that a strictly dominating strategy will be chosen over a dominated one. But even if the player has no idea what the probabilities of the other player's strategies are, the logic of domination is just as compelling.

Weak domination is slightly less powerful. For instance, if player I is Bayesian and is convinced, for some reason, that player II will play $C$ for sure, $C$ will be a best response for him as well as $D$, despite the fact that $D$ weakly dominates $C$. True, he can never lose by switching from $C$ to $D$, but if player II plays $C$, he cannot gain either. Still, it makes sense that weakly dominated strategies will not be played. If the player is not Bayesian and has no clear idea about the choice of the other player, it is safer for him to choose the dominating strategy, even if it is only weakly dominating. This will also be the conclusion of a Bayesian player whose beliefs are not too extreme, allowing a positive probability for each strategy selection by his opponent. Indeed, if we take into account that the other player may, if only by mistake, play any available strategy with some positive probability, however small, then weak domination and strict domination have the same implications.

In games 1 and 2, since there are only two strategies, $D$ dominates every other strategy (because there is only one such other), and it thus qualifies as a *dominant* strategy. Domination is a relation between two strategies, whereas *dominance* is an adjective that applies to a single strategy, meaning that it dominates every other one.

When there are some dominated strategies (for some players) in a game, we may eliminate them and see what happens in the reduced game. Often new dominations appear. For example, in game 2, if we eliminate the strictly dominated strategy (C) of player II, in the reduced game $D$ strictly dominates $C$ for player I. The same can occur with weak domination. Unfortunately, weak domination between strategies of one player may also disappear when we eliminate strategies of other players. On the bright side, this phenomenon cannot occur with strict domination.

When we assume that dominated strategies will not be played, we make a mild assumption regarding the rationality of the players, namely, that it dictates that each player avoid a choice that is dominated according to her own utility function. But when we eliminate dominated strategies and look for new dominations that may arise in the reduced game, we are making additional assumptions about the behavior and reasoning of the players. Iterative elimination of dominated strategies can be justified by the assumption that players are rational and also think that other players are rational, so that it is safe to assume that these others will not play their dominated strategies. Every layer of iterated elimination of dominated strategies assumes another layer of belief that everyone believes that everyone believes that... everyone is rational.

Alternatively, iterative elimination of dominated strategies can be justified if one considers a dynamic process by which dominated strategies are not being played, and over time the fact that they are not chosen is observed by other players, who react optimally to the observed behavior, and so forth. In this case, every layer of iterated elimination requires more time for players to realize that the dominated strategies of the others are not being played. Again, the more layers of iterative elimination of dominated strategies are required for a prediction in a game, the less compelling is the prediction.

### 7.1.3 Back to Prisoner's Dilemma

The claim that players will never play dominated strategies thus requires some qualifications. It may not be entirely compelling when applied to a reduced game obtained from a long sequence of iterative eliminations of dominated strategies. It is less compelling when the notion of domination is weak, especially in iterated elimination. And in large games it is also possible that the players will not notice certain domination pairs.

None of these qualifications applies to prisoner's dilemma. Strategy $D$ dominates strategy $C$. This domination is strict and requires no iterative elimination of dominated strategies. Moreover, the game is about as simple as could be, with only two strategies for each player. Hence, we expect player I to play $D$, and the same applies to player II. It follows that $(D, D)$ will be played, yielding the payoffs $(1, 1)$. But the two players could have chosen $(C, C)$, which would have resulted in the Pareto-superior payoffs $(3, 3)$. Looking at the matrix it is obvious why individual rationality does not necessarily imply group rationality: each player distinguishes between what is under his control and what isn't, as rationality dictates. The row player compares payoffs along columns, realizing that he cannot choose the column. Similarly, the column player compares payoffs across rows, knowing that he cannot choose which row will be played. But then neither gets to compare payoffs along the diagonal. They can look at the matrix and see that $(3, 3)$ is better than $(1, 1)$ for both of them, but neither can make a decision based on this comparison. Neither can decide, single-handedly, to move along the diagonal. It would be irrational for them to compare payoffs along the diagonal. It would be equivalent to wishful thinking, to the belief that they can change that which they cannot.

### 7.1.4 The Meaning of Utility

Prisoner's dilemma is one of the best and worst parables in the social sciences. It is striking in its simplicity. If you have never thought about this problem before, and especially if you tend to believe that people should be left to their own devices, to pursue their own good, this example might change the way you think about social interactions. However, the choice of the story about the prisoners is one of the worst choices that could have been made. The problem is that the story makes one believe that the prisoners don't have any loyalty to each other, that they are heartless and selfish individuals, and that if they had been more altruistic, the problem would have been solved. It has also been argued that game theorists do not understand what motivates people, that they can only conceive of selfish motives, and, worse still, that they preach selfishness. The fact that game theorists get a bad reputation is not very pleasant for anyone who might be known as a game theorist, but in addition this interpretation clouds the main message of prisoner's dilemma. It may make you believe there is no problem here, while in fact there is.

The originators of game theory are not to blame for the poor choice of the prisoners' story. The example was discussed at RAND and Princeton in the 1950s, and it is attributed to Merrill Flood and Melvin Dresher. They were mathematicians, as were the handful of people interested in game theory at the time. This small group realized that the prisoners' story was only a metaphor and that the utility numbers to be put into a game matrix should be the values of the vNM utility function, which is derived from preferences. They could not have imagined how popular the example would become or how much confusion it would generate.

Recall that according to the methodology described in previous chapters, we first observe behavior, then attach utility numbers to the alternatives. Individuals may violate the axioms that are required for such a representation to exist. But if the axioms are not violated, the maximization of utility (or expected utility) is tautological. The utility numbers already incorporate any relevant payoffs—material, psychological, sociological, and so forth. If I play the game with my child, and I prefer to go to jail in his stead, then there will be a higher utility function for me to be in jail and set my child free rather than vice versa. Once we have formulated the game as shown, the inequality $4 > 3$ should mean that after all considerations are taken into account, I prefer defecting even if my partner cooperates. If this is not the case, we should have used different numbers in the game. That is, we would be dealing with a game that is not prisoner's dilemma.

If there were no real life situations for which game 1 was a good model, there would be no problem indeed. Unfortunately, this is not the case. There are situations for which the best simple model does look like game 1, and in such situations we should expect rational individuals to end up in a Pareto-dominated outcome. To see this more clearly, let us consider a different story. You are randomly matched with another person, whom you don't know and will not meet again, to play the following game. Each player goes to a computer screen on which two buttons are drawn. If you touch the first button, the bank will give you a gift of $1,000. If you touch the second button, the bank will give the other player a gift of $3,000. The money comes from the bank, not from your account. The situation is symmetric: the other player will determine whether she gets a gift of $1,000 or you get a gift of $3,000 from the bank. What will you do?

You realize that *whatever the other player is doing right now*, if you touch the first button you will be richer by $1,000. If this is what both players do, they end up with $1,000 each. But they could end up with $3,000 each if each gave the gift to the other. Clearly, if all you care about is money, the game is precisely the same game as stated (with payoffs interpreted as thousands of dollars). For each player, strategy $D$ dominates $C$. In fact, $D$ promises a payoff higher than $C$'s by precisely $1,000. Yet, $(D, D)$ is Pareto-dominated by $(C, C)$.

As in the original prisoner's dilemma, in this story it is also not obvious that the model captures the essence of the situation. It is possible that you don't care only about your own bank account. Perhaps you are altruistic. But then, again, the situation described will not be an example of game 1. The details of the second story were supposed to make the payoffs in game 1 more realistic by minimizing the role of altruism, loyalty, future relationships, and so forth. Perhaps you still do not find game 1 a good model of the proposed story. The claim, however, is that *if* the payoffs in the matrix capture all that matters to the players, *then* the $(D, D)$ prediction relies on very mild assumptions of rationality.

### 7.1.5  Main Lessons

The main point of prisoner's dilemma is that there are many situations of social interaction in which individual rationality does not lead to group rationality. These are situations in which we should think how to change the rules of the game and make it rational for players to play $(C, C)$. It is very dangerous to assume that altruism will take care of the problem. Again, if altruism did suffice, it would have been reflected in the utility functions to begin with. Unfortunately, altruism is not always sufficient.

Some of the greatest mistakes in human history had to do with assumptions that people will be kinder, gentler, and more altruistic than they ended up being. You may or may not like communist ideas, but it is obvious that communism sounds better than it ended up being. If people were to incorporate in their utility functions the well-being of others to a sufficient degree, perhaps communism would have fared better. But the fact is that whenever communism was implemented on a large scale, it was accompanied by secret police. Somehow the lofty ideals of communism did not suffice to implement cooperative behavior. From the point of view of social engineering we could say that the communist ideal suffered from the irrationality discussed in chapter 1. It asked what would be desirable for a society without asking what was feasible, given human nature.

There is no doubt that altruism exists. People do good deeds, volunteer to help, and donate money to worthy causes. Yet, altruism has its limits. Consider the case of public goods such as hospitals, schools, roads, the military—services that serve an entire community. They are called public because all members of the community enjoy benefits from their existence. A unit of a public good can be consumed by many individuals simultaneously. This is in contrast with private goods, such as, say, tomatoes, which cannot be eaten by different people. Typically, we are all better off if we all donate some of our income and get these services than if we all don't donate and have no hospitals and no schools. Public goods are typically provided by public institutions, such as a state or a municipality. They collect taxes in order to finance the public goods. Why is that? Why aren't such services provided by voluntary donations?

The situation is very similar to prisoner's dilemma played among many players. It is true that everyone is better off if everyone donates than if everyone doesn't. Yet, this comparison along the diagonal, as it were, is not the choice faced by any individual. Each individual asks herself, *given* what the others are doing, should I donate money or not? Each can then tell herself, "Whatever is the total donation of the others, the impact of my own donation on the quality of hospitals is minuscule. By contrast, this has been a tough month, and skipping my donation this time might really help me a great deal." As a result, many if not all individuals might decide to opt out, and the public good will not be provided.

Whether public goods should be supported by donations or by the government out of tax revenues depends on many factors, including ideology and culture. In the United States, for instance, much more is left to voluntary donations than in western Europe. Yet, even in the

United States there are federal and state income taxes, and big expenditures (such as the military) are not left to voluntary donations. Importantly, paying these taxes is supported by the threat of penalty. Those who do not pay their taxes may end up in jail.

We should therefore read prisoner's dilemma as a metaphor. It is not about suspects who may decide to betray each other or to be loyal, and it is not about the claim that we should be altruistic or recognize how altruistic people really are. Prisoner's dilemma is about the design of social institutions. It warns us that often we will not obtain a Pareto-optimal outcome unless we change the rules of the game.

### 7.1.6 Changing the Rules of the Game

It would be nice if people played $C$ in game 1. Therefore, we would like it to be rational for people to play $C$. We don't need to make $C$ a dominant strategy; it suffices that it be rational to play $C$ given that the other is playing $C$. To this effect, it would suffice to change one payoff, the 4 in the matrix of game 1. Suppose that if the other player plays $C$ and you play $D$, instead of the enticing 4 you get punished and your utility is $-1$. This punishment becomes the worst payoff in the matrix, but any number lower than 3 would do. Now we have the following game matrix:

**Game 3.   Prisoner's Dilemma with Payoffs Modified by Punishment**

|   | $C$ | $D$ |
|---|---|---|
| $C$ | $(3,3)$ | $(0,-1)$ |
| $D$ | $(-1,0)$ | $(1,1)$ |

In this game, $(C, C)$ is a reasonable prediction. If both players expect the other one to play $C$, it is a best response for both to play $C$. This is called a *Nash equilibrium*.[1] It is still true that if both expect the other to play $D$, they will be better off playing $D$ themselves. That is, $(D, D)$ is also a Nash equilibrium. Yet, $D$ is no longer a dominant strategy, and if we manage somehow to get common expectation to be $(C, C)$, cooperation will be sustained. Taking a normative approach, we can recommend to the players to play $(C, C)$, and such a recommendation would make sense.

How do we change the 4 to a $-1$? One way was already discussed; in the income tax example, legislation is a way to change payoffs. If you do not pay taxes, you will go to jail. This might not be a credible threat if no one pays taxes because jail space is limited. But if everyone else pays taxes, it can be a credible threat, and we can convince people that a pretty low payoff (utility) awaits them if they evade tax payments.

Legislation is often a solution to prisoner's dilemma–type situations. In democratic countries many laws have the features that (1) everyone is better off if everyone follows the law than if everyone doesn't, and (2) everyone is better off if one is exempt from following the law, whether others follow it or not. When such a situation is identified, even a liberal-minded person might support legislation that curbs individual rights.

But laws may be complicated to pass and to enforce. Often, social norms can serve the same purpose at a much lower cost. Suppose you drive down the road and honk or litter. You may be breaching a law, but it can be quite complicated to get you prosecuted and convicted. It is much simpler to frown at you and make you feel antisocial. Thus, the punishment of social reproach can be sufficient to change payoffs and make the cooperative behavior an equilibrium.

To enforce the law we need police and courts of law. To enforce social norms we only need other people. But we can do even better than that. If we change the payoff of defection by generating guilt feelings, we won't even need an external observer to sustain cooperation as an equilibrium. Suppose that when you were a child, your mother told you that it's wrong to litter. Years later, even if no one is around to see you, you may still feel bad if you do litter. Thus, the inculcation of guilt feelings can be an effective way to change payoffs. It can be so effective that you may still feel guilty for littering even if everyone around you does the same.

What is the most effective and least harmful way to enforce cooperation would depend on context. There might also be situations in which the cooperative solution cannot be enforced as equilibrium. But the main lesson is that we should be aware of the possibility of social situations that are of the prisoner's dilemma type and also of the possibility that we may use law, norms, and education to change the payoffs in such situations.

### 7.1.7  Repetition

Another important way of changing the payoffs of a game is to repeat it. If the game is played more than once, the choice of a move (strategy) by a player depends on the history known to her. Hence, when a player contemplates her choice in the present, she has to take into account the possible reactions of others later on, including the possibility of reward and punishment. Once these exist, it is no longer a dominant strategy to defect in the prisoner's dilemma game. In particular, if the other player chooses a strategy that rewards $C$ by playing $C$ herself and punishes $D$ by playing $D$, it may be better to play $C$ at present.

The benefits of repetition of a game, that is, of long-term interaction, are familiar from everyday life. It is not crucial that the players be exactly the same. It suffices that they be drawn from a given population, where there is a non-negligible probability of encountering the same player again or encountering someone who encountered someone who encountered...someone who played with this player. In this case, if other players may start punishing their partners by playing $D$, such reactions may spread and get back to the player who first played $D$. One may then find that it doesn't pay to violate the social norm of playing $C$ for a one-time gain. If, however, the population is very large, so that the probability of meeting the same player again (or anyone who has met anyone who has met...the same player) is very small, one may be tempted to reap the one-time payoff of $D$, realizing that it has little or no effect on future payoffs.

One lesson we learn from this way of thinking is that when there is a temptation to behave selfishly and noncooperatively, cooperative behavior is easier to sustain in small groups than in large ones. In quiet suburbs people tend to drive differently than in large cities. When we have a higher chance of meeting the same individuals again, we tend to respect their rights more than in one-shot interactions. If a kitchen is being used by only a few colleagues, it is more likely to be kept clean than if it is used by hundreds of people.

Based on the same intuition, if we think of $C$ as contributing to society as much as we can and of $D$ as shirking, we also find that communism would work in small communes better than in large ones. Indeed, Israeli kibbutzim remained true to the communist ideals much longer than any communist country. When a few hundred people are involved, repetition helps sustain the cooperative strategy. When millions of people are involved, the temptations of shirking are larger, and secret police are more likely to be relied upon to support the ideals.

### 7.1.8 Kant's Categorical Imperative and the Golden Rule
Kant suggested that one's moral philosophy should be dictated by the categorical imperative: "Act only according to that maxim whereby

you can at the same time will that it should become a universal law."[2] While Kant's philosophy is beyond the scope of this book, I discuss the practical counterpart of the categorical imperative, which is a rather intuitive criterion for moral judgment. When a child is too noisy, he may hear, "Imagine what would happen if everyone were as noisy as you are." For want of a better name, and in honor of Kant, I still refer to it as the categorical imperative (CI).

The CI could be viewed as attempting to change the payoff of 4 in the original prisoner's dilemma matrix (game 1). If you are about to play $D$ and expect to enjoy the high payoff, Kant urges you to think what would happen if everyone played $D$ and you'd get only 1. Alternatively, we can think of the consequence that involves a high material payoff but a violation of a general rule.

It is important to realize that accepting the CI is a moral choice that we make, to forgo the payoff of 4 *as if* it led to 1. Clearly, when one player chooses $D$, it *does not follow* that the other player does the same. When we draw a game matrix, it is implicitly understood that these are two sovereign and causally independent decision makers. It would be a mistake to think that if you play $D$, so will the other player. This would be true if you were playing with your mirror image, in which case the game would look as follows:

**Game 4.   Prisoner's Dilemma Played with the Mirror Image**

Reflection

| | |
|---|---|
| $C$ | $(3,3)$ |
| $D$ | $(1,1)$ |

That is, the row player (you) can make a choice between $C$ and $D$, knowing that the mirror image will do the same. In this case $C$ is clearly dominant. But this is not the game we are playing. We are looking at two independent decision makers, and the CI can be viewed as attempting to change their payoffs despite the fact that they are not causally related.

It is worthy of note that the CI involves a process of induction—judging a particular deed as an instance of a universal law. But the applicability as well as the moral validity of the CI is limited because it is not always obvious what the appropriate generalization is. To consider a trivial example, suppose I wonder whether it would be ethical for me to have coffee in my living room. It seems obvious that the appropriate generalization is "everyone is having coffee in *their* living room" rather than, say, "everyone is having coffee in *my* living room." But sometimes the appropriate generalization is less obvious. Suppose we attempt to judge the moral status of the European immigration to the Americas. One possible generalization would be "every nation with a superior technology invades another nation's country and conquers it." Another is "every hungry or persecuted individual seeks to move to a free and less populated land." Both rules can be argued to be generalizing the particular instance, but our willingness to accept them is quite different. The difficulty is that often an argument for or against a certain deed may be incorporated into its description, so that a generalization to a universal law will include only cases in which this argument holds. In this sense, the CI as a guiding principle is not always helpful is solving moral dilemmas.

The CI is still helpful in reminding us that our moral judgment should not depend on our own identity. Whatever we consider moral should be generalizable across individuals, and we should not judge ourselves differently than others. In this sense, the CI is reminiscent of the Golden Rule, which can be summarized as "treat others as you would like to be treated." The Golden Rule appeared in Greek philosophy as well as in other ancient cultures. Again, it is an attempt to change one's payoffs by imagining a hypothetical situation. The Golden Rule asks us to imagine only a reversal of roles, whereas Kant's CI asks us to imagine a situation in which everyone does the same as we do. Thus, the cognitive task required by the CI is more demanding; we are asked to imagine a situation that might not be similar to anything we have seen. Both, however, are ways to change payoffs and can be viewed as definitions of the utility one *should* use rather than the utility one actually uses.

## 7.2 Nash Equilibria

### 7.2.1 Definition
As previously mentioned, a selection of strategies for players is a *Nash equilibrium* if the strategy of each player is a best response to the selection of strategies of the others. (See appendix B for formal definitions and a statement of Nash's result.)

### 7.2.2 Justifications
Why is the notion of a Nash equilibrium interesting? Why should we believe that players will play a Nash equilibrium? It makes sense that

each player will take the other players' choices as independent of his own and maximize his utility given these constraints. This is basically what constrained optimization dictates. But how would a player know what the others are going to play?

There are several ways in which such knowledge or belief may arise. One is history. Suppose the game is played over and over again, with different players selected at random from large populations to play the game each time. Thus, there exists a long history from which players can learn. At the same time, players wish to play optimally at each round because the probability of being matched with the same players in the future is negligible. That is, this is not a repeated game in which a player might expect long-term effects such as reward or retaliation. Suppose, further, that in this setup we find that the same strategies are being played every time over a long history. It would appear strange if the strategies did not constitute a Nash equilibrium. When history is sufficiently regular we expect players (1) to learn what the others are doing, and (2) to respond optimally to it. Thus, a Nash equilibrium seems to be a minimal requirement on a selection of strategies to be played over and over again when players are randomly selected from large populations.

Another scenario in which a Nash equilibrium is expected to result is when a coordinator suggests to the players a way to play the game. Suppose the players get the recommendation together and then go their own way and choose what to play independently. If the recommendation failed to be a Nash equilibrium, we would not be surprised to see that it isn't followed. It seems that for a recommendation to be followed, it should satisfy the minimal condition that if the players believe it is going to be followed by others, they wish to follow it themselves. This is basically what a Nash equilibrium is.

It is important to point out, however, that in the absence of history, a coordinator, or another correlation device, it is not entirely clear why a Nash equilibrium will be played. Moreover, history may not exhibit any convergence to a Nash equilibrium, and we have no general results on reasonable dynamic processes that converge to equilibria.

If all we are equipped with are the assumptions that players are rational, that they know that others are, that they know that others know it, and so on, we end up with a solution concept called rationalizability, a concept introduced by Douglas Bernheim and David Pearce in the 1980s.[3] A strategy is *rationalizable* if it is a best response to some Bayesian beliefs about other players' choices, where these beliefs have to be compatible with the other players' also choosing best responses to some beliefs, which are, in turn, also restricted to strategies that are best responses to some beliefs, and so on. A Nash equilibrium identifies a rationalizable strategy for each player. The player chooses a best response to his beliefs, and these beliefs are assumed to be correct. In particular, a player's beliefs about the others is that they choose optimal strategies given their own (correct) beliefs. However, a selection of a rationalizable strategy for each player need not be a Nash equilibrium because the concept of rationalizability does not presuppose that beliefs are correct or common to all players.

### 7.2.3 Mixed Strategies

A classic game called matching pennies involves two players who simultaneously pull coins out of their pockets. Each can choose a side of the coin, $H$ or $T$, and player I wins if and only if the two coins show the same side. Suppose that they play for one dollar. The game is the following:

**Game 5.   Matching Pennies**

|       | $H$      | $T$      |
|-------|----------|----------|
| $H$   | $(1,-1)$ | $(-1,1)$ |
| $T$   | $(-1,1)$ | $(1,-1)$ |

It is easy to see that this game has no Nash equilibrium among the choices $(H,H)$, $(H,T)$, $(T,H)$, $(T,T)$. It also makes sense intuitively; whatever one suggests as a play of the game, there will be a player who is about to lose a dollar and who can change the outcome to gaining a dollar by changing (only) her own choice.

This is reminiscent of many real games, such as parlor and sports games. For example, think of a penalty kick in soccer, where the row player can choose where to kick the ball, and the column player, the goalie, can choose where to jump. Assuming that each has only two choices, and that their decisions are made simultaneously (in particular, the goalie has to decide where to jump before he can watch the ball, if he wants to have a chance at getting it), the game is similar to the game 5 matrix. Indeed, there could be no equilibrium in such a game. If both players know what is going to be played, one of them will have an incentive to choose a different strategy.

What happens in such games? Players try to be unpredictable so as not to be outguessed. We can model this by assuming that players

randomize. Their choices need not be truly random; they only need to
appear random to others. The choice of a strategy according to a random device is referred to as a *mixed strategy*. The original, deterministic
strategies are referred to as *pure*.

Once players are allowed to randomize, how do they rank random
payoffs? The standard assumption is that they maximize the expected
payoff, as suggested by the vNM theorem. To be precise, if the players
satisfy the vNM axioms, we should use their vNM utility functions to
model the game. It then follows that they will maximize the expected
value of the numbers in the game matrix. With this assumption, Nash
has proved that (Nash) equilibria always exist, that is, every finite
game has at least one Nash equilibrium.

There are several interpretations of Nash equilibrium with mixed
strategies that are more or less the counterparts of the interpretations
of probability discussed previously. The simplest interpretation, corresponding to the notion of empirical frequencies, has to do with choices
in a game that is repeated over and over again, where the players are
randomly drawn at each stage from large populations. Consider a
given player at a particular stage in the game. She asks, What are the
other players likely to do? and What is my best choice, given that?

The assumption of random matching suggests simple answers to
both questions. First, having observed the past choices of other players
in similar conditions, the player can use the frequencies of choices in
the past as a reasonable definition of the probability of choice in the
next stage. Second, since the player realizes that she is unlikely to be
matched with the same players again in the near future, she has an incentive to maximize her expected stage payoff, ignoring long-run considerations such as rewards or punishments.

If the game is played repeatedly by the same players, a player
should not only ask what would be the short-term outcome of possible
strategies but also what would be their impact on future stages. As a
result, the game should be conceived of as a single play of a large
game in which there are many stages.

In the absence of history, players may use subjective probability, and
this corresponds to an interpretation of Nash equilibrium as "equilibrium in beliefs." This interpretation suggests that a mixed strategy does
not represent actual randomization by the player; rather, it reflects the
beliefs of the other players about her choice. The equilibrium concept
implicitly assumes that these beliefs are shared by all players. Moreover, if we wish to interpret the equilibrium as a prediction about
actual play, we need to assume also that these beliefs are correct.

The existence of Nash equilibria is important from a theoretical point of view. Yet, a few qualifications are in order. First, existence of mixed equilibria does not provide a refutable prediction for one-shot games. A mixed equilibrium may be interpreted as average frequency of play over many repetitions, but it does not specify what we should expect to observe in a single play. Second, as mentioned for pure strategy Nash equilibria, there is no general result that guarantees that a reasonable dynamic process would converge to a Nash equilibrium. Finally, on the bright side, a general existence result is not always needed for applications. For example, we can consider Nash equilibria in pure strategies. We know that they need not always exist. But if we consider a game that has such an equilibrium, we may use this prediction, and our trust in it need not depend on general existence results.

## 7.3    Equilibrium Selection

Now that we know that Nash equilibria exist, it would be nice to know that they are unique. If they were, the notion of equilibrium would provide a well-defined prediction for every game. Unfortunately, Nash equilibria are not unique. We begin with a few very simple examples in two-person games and then continue with more realistic examples with more players.

### 7.3.1    Stylized Examples
To consider the simplest of examples, suppose we have to decide whether to drive on the right or on the left. Let's focus on a single interaction between two cars approaching each other on the road. The game may be modeled as follows:

**Game 6.    Pure Coordination 1**

|     | $R$       | $L$       |
| --- | --------- | --------- |
| $R$ | $(1,1)$   | $(0,0)$   |
| $L$ | $(0,0)$   | $(1,1)$   |

Both drivers are alive (payoff of 1) if they choose the same driving side, and they are in bad shape (payoff of 0) if they choose different driving sides. In this game both $(R, R)$ and $(L, L)$ are pure strategy equilibria, and both are played in reality (e.g., in the U.S. and the U.K.). Obviously, there is complete symmetry between the two strategies, and we cannot hope for any theoretical consideration to choose one equilibrium over the other.

Observe that this is a game of pure coordination. There is no conflict of interest between the two players. They just want to be coordinated. Yet, they may not be coordinated and end up crashing. It would therefore be useful to have a law that dictates on which side of the road one should drive. Here the role of the law is not to solve a prisoner's dilemma type of situation but to serve as a coordination device.

Pure coordination games might have Nash equilibria that are not equivalent in the eyes of the players. Suppose, for example, that players I and II wish to meet, and they can each go to restaurant $A$ or to restaurant $B$. Both prefer $A$ to $B$, but their main goal is to get together. If they do not meet each other, they'll skip dinner. The game might look as follows:

**Game 7.  Pure Coordination 2**

|       | $A$     | $B$     |
|-------|---------|---------|
| $A$   | $(3,3)$ | $(0,0)$ |
| $B$   | $(0,0)$ | $(1,1)$ |

Again, we have two pure strategy Nash equilibria. We might hope that the players will be smart enough to coordinate on $A$, but if, for whatever reason, they came to believe that the meeting was set to $B$, they both have an incentive to go to $B$. Here we could expect a law or regulation not only to help the players coordinate but also to exclude the Pareto-dominated equilibrium, thus eliminating the "bad" option from their choices.

Games that are not pure coordination can still have an aspect of coordination as well as of competition. For example, the "battle of the sexes" is a story of a couple, very much in love with each other, who have to decide whether to go to the ballet or a boxing match. Importantly, the choices are made individually. Neither would enjoy any show on their own, but, given that they are going to meet, they have different tastes. The game can be modeled as follows:

**Game 8.  Battle of the Sexes**

|        | Ballet  | Boxing  |
|--------|---------|---------|
| Ballet | $(2,1)$ | $(0,0)$ |
| Boxing | $(0,0)$ | $(1,2)$ |

(The woman is the row player, and the man is the column player, if you are willing to stick to gender stereotypes.) Here, again, we have two pure strategy Nash equilibria, which are differently ranked by the two players.

In each of games 6, 7, and 8 there is also a mixed strategy equilibrium, but such an equilibrium is not a very reasonable prediction in these games. If one perturbs the beliefs a little bit, one finds that the best response leads to one of the pure strategy Nash equilibria rather than back to the mixed one.

Finally, consider the following stag hunt game (inspired by a metaphor of Jean-Jacques Rousseau). Two people go into the forest to hunt. Each can go after a hare or a stag. A stag is a better prize, but it requires the collaboration of both. A hare isn't a lot of food, but each hunter can get a hare on his own. The game can be modeled as follows:

**Game 9. Stag Hunt**

|  | Stag | Hare |
|---|---|---|
| Stag | $(10, 10)$ | $(0, 7)$ |
| Hare | $(7, 0)$ | $(7, 7)$ |

Both $(Stag, Stag)$ and $(Hare, Hare)$ are pure strategy Nash equilibria. The former Pareto-dominates the latter. But, as opposed to a pure coordination game, the Pareto-dominating equilibrium is riskier. If you go for a stag, and your colleague goes for a hare, you're going to starve. If there is a doubt about whether the other player will indeed play his equilibrium strategy, you may start thinking about the hare. And the fact that your colleague might be having the exact same thoughts might only encourage you to switch to the safer option, the hare. In a term coined by John Harsanyi and Reinhard Selten, $(Hare, Hare)$ *risk-dominates* $(Stag, Stag)$ because it is optimal given a wider set of beliefs about the behavior of the other player.[4]

### 7.3.2 Real-Life Examples

**Revolutions** Consider a country in which there is a totalitarian regime, which is disliked by the vast majority of the citizens. The regime relies on the military and the secret police, and if a few citizens engage in illegal activities, they will be punished. But if a large enough portion of the population joins an insurgence, the regime will be overthrown. Viewed as a game among the citizens, each having two options, rebel and acquiesce, there are two pure strategy Nash equilibria. The transition from one to the other is what we call a revolution or a coup d'état.

In reality, some attempts to topple regimes succeed and some fail. That is, when the political system is perturbed, it sometimes settles on one equilibrium and sometimes on another. We often find it hard to predict which equilibrium will be played.

**Bank Runs**  Banks are based on the idea that people deposit their money and ask to withdraw it when they need it. If times of withdrawal are random, the bank can keep only a portion of the deposits and invest the rest. If, for some reason, all clients show up one morning and ask for their money, the bank will not be able to pay them and will go bankrupt.

Should the bank's clients ask for their money? It depends. If they tend to believe that others won't, then the bank is financially stable, and there is no need to withdraw the money. It's actually better to leave it in the bank and earn some interest. But if the clients believe that other clients are about to withdraw their money, they realize that the bank is in danger of bankruptcy, and it then makes sense to withdraw the money, preferably fast. This leads to a phenomenon of a bank run; people rush to be among the first to withdraw their deposits while the bank still has some money.

This situation can be viewed as a game with many players and two pure strategy equilibria: one in which everyone trusts the bank, and then everyone has a good reason to trust the bank, and another in which no one does, and then everyone has a good reason not to. The selection of equilibrium here is crucial; it is the difference between financial stability and a financial crisis.

**Respecting the Law**  Suppose that a new antismoking law is being passed. It may be respected, but it may also be ignored. In many countries there are laws that exist on paper but are never enforced. What will be the fate of a new law?

As in the previous examples, there are two reasonable equilibria in the game. If everyone follows the law, a single individual who violates it is likely to be penalized, and thus obeying the law is an equilibrium. If, however, everyone ignores the law, the state does not have the resources to penalize every violation, and it is then a best response for an individual to ignore the law.

**Conclusion**  In all these examples each equilibrium is a self-fulfilling prophecy. The choice of equilibrium cannot be made based on theoretical considerations alone. One needs to understand culture and history in order to make predictions regarding the equilibrium that will end up being played. Game theory provides us with a powerful tool to clarify our thinking and trim down the set of scenarios that might materialize, but it does not come up with a single prediction. Analytical thinking is tremendously helpful in identifying the set of reasonable eventualities, but it cannot replace acquaintance with history, understanding of institutional details, or intuition.

## 7.4 The Power of Commitment

Consider the battle of the sexes (game 8) again. The game has two pure strategy Nash equilibria, each preferred by one of the players to the other equilibrium. Assume now that the man, who is the column player, puts on his running shoes and leaves the house. Interpret this move as a unilateral commitment of the player not to go to the ballet (where running shoes will be unacceptable). That is, the man eliminates one of his choices. What will happen next? The woman, knowing that the man cannot go to the ballet, faces the following reduced game:

**Game 10. Battle of the Sexes after Elimination of One Column**

|  | Boxing |
|---|---|
| Ballet | $(0,0)$ |
| Boxing | $(1,2)$ |

Her best response is to go to the boxing match. Evidently, this is the Nash equilibrium preferred by the column player in the original game. Thus, we find that he can benefit from commitment; by eliminating one of his strategies, we changed the game. Rather than having a game with two pure Nash equilibria, he generated a new game in which there is only one equilibrium. Instead of having some uncertainty about which equilibrium will be played, if at all, the player imposed his preferred equilibrium on his partner.

Before proceeding, a comment is due. Game-theoretic analysis assumes that the game under discussion describes all relevant moves by all players. Hence, if indeed a player can eliminate some of his strategies, or send signals to the other players, or do anything else that can change the nature of the game, these moves should be a priori introduced into the game. In the ballet/boxing example, if the man does indeed have a choice between putting on his running shoes and disappearing or staying and negotiating, this choice should be described as part of the game, presumably as a first step before the play of the battle of the sexes. In other words, the battle of the sexes as described in game 8 implicitly assumes that no additional moves are possible by the players. The game with running shoes is a different game despite the fact that in certain stages it resembles game 8.

The fact that a player may benefit from elimination of possible alternatives is peculiar. In a one-person decision problem we did not encounter this phenomenon; a player who is rational in the classic sense can only benefit from more options. Indeed, if she doesn't like the additional options, she is free not to select them. One could have exceptions due to cognitive limitations or to problems of self-control. But a classically rational player cannot suffer from the addition of alternatives nor benefit from their elimination.

By contrast, in a strategic interaction one may benefit from elimination of alternatives, or equivalently, from committing to choose a strategy in a given subset. The player in fact does not benefit from having fewer options per se. He benefits from the fact that the others *know* that he is not going to choose the eliminated options.

The power of commitment is familiar from international politics. Consider a fragile peace between two nuclear superpowers A and B. A might attack B in a limited way, and then B will have to decide whether to respond, risking further escalation, or negotiate a new peaceful agreement. If B is rational, it may prefer the latter alternative, if indeed attacked. Since A knows that, it may be tempted to attack for the immediate gain, trusting that B will be rational enough not to try to punish A, thereby risking further escalation. Now assume that B considers the installation of an automatic retaliation system, which would respond to any attack without further decisions being made by the player. Such a system is tantamount to a commitment to a certain strategy (of response), that is, to an elimination of some of the player's strategies. But this commitment may be beneficial because it reduces A's incentive to attack in the first place.

Along similar lines, commitment to vulnerability can also be beneficial. Consider the same example, and suppose that B may install a missile defense system that would greatly reduce, but not eliminate, A's ability to hurt B. B knows that the installation of such a system would make it less costly to attack, and that, knowing this, A may wish to preempt an attack by B. By contrast, if B remains vulnerable, it signals to $A$ that it has no aggressive intentions, thereby reducing $A$'s incentive to strike first.

## 7.5 Common Knowledge

The discussion of Nash equilibrium in general, and of equilibrium selection in particular, touches on issues of knowledge or belief about the world, including the other players in the game. Reasoning about what these players will do, one has to think what they know or believe, and one finds that they are thinking about other players as well. Pretty soon one realizes that it is important to know what players believe that other players believe that other players believe, and so forth.

A fact is called *common knowledge* among a set of individuals if everyone knows it, everyone knows that everyone knows it, and so on. This concept was developed in philosophy by David Lewis (late 1960s), in game theory by Robert Aumann (mid-1970s), and in computer science by Joseph Halpern and Yoram Moses (early 1980s).[5] Lewis was interested in social conventions, Aumann in equilibria in games, and Halpern and Moses in coordination among computers.

When we think about equilibrium play, we realize that in order to justify why rational players would play it, we resort to something that is quite close to common knowledge. A rational player will play an equilibrium strategy if he thinks that the others are going to play their respective strategies. We don't need more than this single layer of belief in order to justify the equilibrium. But if the other players are also supposed to be reasoning entities, we may ask the player why he thinks that the others will play their equilibrium strategies. And he would probably say, "Because they are rational and do what is a best response for them," but this means that he believes that these other players also believe that this equilibrium will be played. And if we delve deeper and ask why he thinks that these other players so think, we become interested in his third-order beliefs, namely, what he believes the other players believe that other players believe, and so forth.

## 7.6 Extensive Form Games

The games described in previous sections were defined by matrices, where rows and columns described strategies and the matrix specified the utility functions. This formulation can be extended to more than two players. It is referred to as the *normal form* or *strategic form* of the game. It lists all strategies without describing the dynamics of the game.

Another way to model games follows the chronological order of the moves by the players. In this *extensive form*, the game is described by a tree, where at each node a particular player is assigned to play, and the edges coming out of the node describe the various moves that the player can make. (See figures 7.1 and 7.2 in the next section.) This depiction of a game is particularly appealing when the game has a clear chronological unfolding.

If the game is not so clearly structured chronologically, and some players make some decisions simultaneously, the extensive form can still be used to model the game with the addition of information sets. An *information set* is a set of nodes of a particular player that are indistinguishable as far as that player is concerned when called upon to play. That is, if the player is actually at one of the nodes in an information set, she knows that she is at one of those nodes but not which one.

If players always know at which node they are, namely, they know precisely what other players played before them, we say that the game is of *perfect information*. (This means that each information set contains only one element.) Such games include chess, checkers, tic-tac-toe, and other parlor games in which no element of chance is involved. Perfect information games also often appear as models of strategic interactions between countries, firms, or individuals.

Any strategic interaction can be modeled either as a game in the normal form or in the extensive form. There are standard ways to transform a game from the normal to the extensive form, and vice versa. Basic concepts such as dominated strategies and Nash equilibria can be defined in the extensive form model in equivalent ways to their respective definitions in the normal form model.

## 7.7 Perfectness and Credible Threats

Consider the following situation. You are walking down a deserted dark alley. Suddenly you feel a hard pointed object pushed against your back, and a voice says, "Your money or your life." What do you do?

You can think of this situation as an extensive form game. You are player I, who can decide to give his wallet or not. You don't know

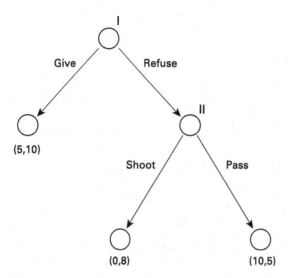

Figure 7.1

who the robber is and whether he has a loaded gun. For simplicity, assume that he does and that the only uncertainty is strategic: will he use
it? Think of the robber as player II. To simplify the problem further, assume he has no incentive to shoot you if you give your wallet. Thus, if
you give the wallet, the game ends in an outcome that is best for the
robber. For you (player I) this outcome is worse than keeping your
money and not being shot, but better than being shot. This situation is
modeled in figure 7.1 as an extensive form game. The game starts after
the pointed object has already been felt on your back. You now have
two options. The option Give yields a payoff of 5 to you and 10 to the
robber. If you refuse, the robber (player II) can choose to shoot you
and take the wallet, or to pass. If he shoots you, your payoff will be 0
and his will be 8. If he passes, you will get a payoff of 10 (keeping
your wallet *and* your life), and he will get a payoff of 5.

When you consider what to do, you're likely to think about the robber's strategy. Suppose you don't give your wallet. What will the
robber do? You realize he can shoot you and take the wallet out of
your pocket himself. The point of the story is that this is a better outcome for him than walking away without the money. Hence, the robber's threat, "Your money or your life," is credible; it is the choice of
the strategy Shoot, which is a best response to player I's strategy Refuse. However, player I's strategy Refuse is not a best response to

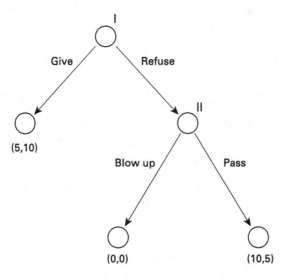

Figure 7.2

player II's strategy Shoot. Given that player II intends to shoot, player I's best response is Give. And for player II, Shoot is a best reply also to Give because if Give is selected by player I, player II does not have a chance to play, and whatever he does is optimal. In short, the pair of strategies Give and Shoot constitutes a Nash equilibrium. In fact, this is the only Nash equilibrium in this game in pure strategies.

Next, consider the same example with the modification that the robber is not equipped with a gun but with a hand grenade. He stands behind you, saying, "If you don't give me the wallet, I'll blow you up." But it is clear to both of you that the technology of hand grenades is such that both of you will be blown up in this case. The game is depicted in figure 7.2. The only difference between this game and that of figure 7.1 is that Shoot, yielding payoffs $(0,8)$, was replaced by Blow up, with payoff $(0,0)$. Will you give your wallet in this game?

Reinhard Selten suggested distinguishing between credible and noncredible threats using his notions of *subgame perfect* and *perfect* equilibria (introduced in the 1960s and 1970s).[6] In the first example (with the gun), the robber's threat to kill you is credible. If he has to carry it out, he has an incentive to do so. Restricting attention to the subgame that would result from your refusal to give your wallet, it is a best response for the robber to shoot you, as specified by his equilibrium strategy. Selten called this a subgame perfect equilibrium because it is an equilibrium of the entire game, and the restriction of equilibrium strategies to each subgame (starting from a given node in the tree) also results in an equilibrium in this subgame.

By contrast, in the second (hand grenade) example, the threat is not credible. If the robber has to carry it out, he would have an incentive to reconsider his threat and stay alive rather than blowing both of you up. Importantly, the Nash equilibrium of the first game (with the gun) is also an equilibrium of the second game. Your strategy Give is a best response to his strategy Blow up because, knowing that the robber plans to blow up the hand grenade if you refuse to give the wallet, it is a best response for you to give the wallet. The robber's strategy is also a best response to yours because, knowing that you will give the wallet, the robber loses nothing by his blow-up threat.

But there is something artificial in this Nash equilibrium. The robber's strategy is a best response to yours only because he is never called upon to actually play it. In fact, his hand grenade threat is not credible. If he finds himself choosing between blowing up both of you or not, he will prefer not to. Knowing this in advance, you may call his bluff. You can deviate from your equilibrium strategy and say, "I'm not giving you the wallet; let's see if you really intend to blow us both up!" The fact that this threat is not credible is captured by the notion of subgame perfectness. If we restrict the Nash equilibrium strategies to the subgame starting from the node in which player II has to move, we find that in this subgame his strategy is not optimal for him. Thus, the Nash equilibrium in which you give your wallet is not subgame perfect.

### 7.7.1 Backward Induction

Games of perfect information can be analyzed by *backward induction*. We start at the leaves of the tree and work backward. At each stage we ask what the player would do at a given node, assuming we have already solved the remainder of the tree. Since no uncertainty is involved, the player's choice is well defined, up to breaking ties. That is, we may not get a unique prediction if the player has to choose among several options that yield the same payoff to her. We may still care about the way she makes her decision because the outcomes that are equivalent in her eyes may be different for the other players. If, however, all payoffs differ from each other, the backward induction procedure provides a unique prediction.

In an intuitive sense, the backward induction solution relies on common knowledge of rationality, understood to imply maximization of one's own utility when the outcome of each choice is known. When we are at the end of the tree and have to predict a player's choice between alternatives under conditions of certainty, it suffices to assume rationality of that player in order to predict that she will choose the leaf that promises her the highest payoff. In fact, if we model the interaction correctly, the payoff should be a utility function that describes choices, and the maximization of this function is tautological.

When we climb one step up, we need to assume that the player who makes the choice is rational but also that he believes that the player who plays after him is rational. Without such a belief, our analysis of behavior at the last decision node may not be shared by the player who plays before it. When we climb one more layer up, in order to justify the backward induction solution we need to assume that the player whose turn it is to play is rational, that he knows that those playing after him are rational, and that he knows that they know that those playing after them are rational. And on it goes. It is easy to see that in order to justify the backward induction solution, we need to assume that the number of layers of knowledge of rationality is at least as large as the depth of the tree.

Common knowledge of rationality need not give us a unique predictionin games in general. But it is widely believed that in (finite) extensive form games of perfect information, if all payoffs differ from each other (for each player), common knowledge of rationality leads to a unique prediction, which is the backward induction solution.[7] Indeed, in these games the backward induction solution is the unique subgame perfect equilibrium, and also the unique selection of strategies that results from iterative elimination of weakly dominated strategies.

# 8 Free Markets

## 8.1 Example: The Case for Globalization

*Olivier*: I hate what's happening to this country. It doesn't feel like France anymore.

*Paul*: What do you mean?

*Olivier*: Everything is produced elsewhere. Nothing is real. Anything you can think of is produced in China or Korea.

*Paul*: And what's wrong with that?

*Olivier*: It's just not my country anymore. Apart from cheeses, thank God, which they still haven't figured out how to import.

*Paul*: And ...?

*Olivier*: You know, wherever you go it feels like the country's being taken over by foreigners.

*Paul*: I see. You mean that there are too many immigrants.

*Olivier*: There are a lot, that's for sure.

*Paul*: So what's really bothering you is not that they sew clothes in China. What's bothering you is that there are too many non-French people around. I suspected as much.

*Olivier*: Look here, I always vote right-wing, but I'm not racist. Don't try to make me out to be one.

*Paul*: I still don't understand what your problem is. It sounds very much like *La France aux francais*. ["France for the French," a right-wing election slogan.]

*Olivier*: As far as I recall, you were never a great supporter of globalization either.

*Paul*:   Sure, but for very different reasons.

*Olivier*:   Such as?

*Paul*:   It's terrible to see what the Western world is doing to developing countries. It's colonization all over again. The idea is to get cheap labor, poor kids working for pitiful salaries.

*Olivier*:   Okay, that, too. A very bad practice.

*Paul*:   Plus, capitalism and consumerism are making us all the same. Wherever you go, you find Starbucks and Nike and, of course, McDonald's. First all the airports looked the same, now all the cities look the same, wherever you are in the world. No variety, no richness of experience. We're all like automated consumers who march according to the tunes of the market.

*Olivier*:   So, you see, you hate globalization, too.

*Paul*:   Yes, but I hate it because I love people, not because I hate them. I object to globalization because it erases and flattens cultures, not because, like you, I prefer to keep those cultures away.

[*Michel enters.*]

*Michel*:   Oh, you two are denigrating globalization again, eh?

*Olivier*:   Well, it's a very bad thing, let me tell you. And it's going to be our ruin.

*Michel*:   At least you have this in common with the rest of the world. It's quite impressive that the same arguments against globalization appear everywhere around the globe.

*Paul*:   So maybe they are convincing.

*Michel*:   But so are the counterarguments. The arguments apparently do not depend on nationality as much as on profession.

*Paul*:   You mean that all economists around the world have been brainwashed to sing the praise of globalization.

*Michel*:   Not quite all. But it is true that they at least know what the argument *for* globalization is.

*Olivier*:   And what is it? Enlighten us!

*Michel*:   It's quite simple, but not always obvious. The point is that if you let people trade—*let*, not *force*—you allow them to do things that improve the conditions of all parties involved. And this works whether you think of buying clothes or buying labor, whether you import the final goods or whether people emigrate. Markets are efficient.

*Paul*: I hate this notion of efficiency. I don't want to be efficient and to run around all day long. I want to have time to think and feel and be myself.

*Michel*: That's fine, but it's not the kind of efficiency I'm talking about.

*Paul*: What other kinds of efficiency are there?

*Michel*: Economists think about Pareto efficiency, named after Pareto. The idea of efficiency is not to produce or consume more. The idea is only not to miss opportunities to make some people better off without hurting others.

*Olivier*: That sounds impossible. You always hurt someone.

*Michel*: Slowly. I'm trying to define, actually, what is inefficient. It is inefficient to be in a situation where you can, without any cost to anyone, strictly improve the utility of some. And you will be surprised, this inefficiency can happen and it happens every day.

*Paul*: For example?

*Michel*: Whenever you pay taxes. Suppose that your kitchen sink is leaking and you call a plumber. You're willing to pay 100 euros for the leak to be fixed, and the guy is willing to fix it for that amount.

*Olivier*: Cool. Especially if he's French.

*Michel*: Only there is one problem. The plumber pays income tax, let's say 50 percent of his income. So he needs to charge you 200 euros to be left with the 100 euros that would make it worthwhile for him to do the job.

*Paul*: So I pay him 200?

*Michel*: Maybe you do. But there is a point where you'll think, that's too expensive, I'll try to fix it myself.

*Paul*: Great. It will do you no harm to do some honest work from time to time.

*Michel*: But this should be your decision. The point is that if you allowed the two people to trade, they would have traded, say, at 100 euros, and both would be happier. No one on earth would be hurt.

*Olivier*: But there is an income tax. Why should I pay it and the plumber shouldn't?

*Michel*: Yes, we have to collect taxes, and plumbers should pay them as well. Still, you can see why the government's involvement can lead to a situation that is *not* Pareto-efficient. Because of taxes, a trade that could have taken place and would have made all parties better off at no cost to anyone else, doesn't take place.

*Paul*:   And the same is true of globalization?

*Michel*:   In principle. That is, someone can produce a shirt for a low cost in a developing country, and someone is willing to pay for it much more than the cost, and if you oppose globalization, you simply don't let them trade.

*Paul*:   So you're saying that imposing constraints on trade will bring us to a bad outcome, one that is not Pareto-efficient, is that it?

*Michel*:   Yes.

*Paul*:   Sounds like the old arguments by Adam Smith and David Ricardo.

*Michel*:   Old doesn't mean wrong.

*Paul*:   So you think that if we remove all barriers to trade we'll be in a better position?

*Michel*:   Not automatically, but we will be in a Pareto-efficient allocation. One that cannot be improved upon in everyone's eyes.

*Olivier*:   But it won't be a better allocation, as you call it, as compared to the old one. If the shirt is now much cheaper, and a good French tailor is out of business, he's not better off.

*Michel*:   It is a bit delicate. The new allocation cannot be improved upon, but that doesn't mean it's better than *any* allocation that can be improved upon. In order to make the tailor better off, you do need to compensate him. But you can do it because if we let the less expensive producers produce the good, we have enough left over to compensate the more expensive ones.

*Olivier*:   What do you mean by *compensate*?

*Michel*:   Give them money.

*Paul*:   I've never seen this done.

*Michel*:   Well, I have. For instance, you have welfare for the unemployed.

*Olivier*:   Wonderful. Send them back home, sitting and waiting for their welfare checks. A great solution indeed.

*Paul*:   Olivier's right. You can't compensate them with money. You take a very restricted economic viewpoint. You don't think about individual self-esteem and the fiber of society. You studied economics, but you evidently never opened a book in psychology or sociology.

*Michel*: Hey, one at a time. I told you that not all economists are for globalization. But I think you should at least understand the basic reasoning before you start criticizing it. I'm not quite sure you understand it. I'm not quite sure you really *want* to understand it. [*Leaves the room angrily.*]

*Paul* [*looking at Olivier and rolling his eyes*]: These economists. They will never learn how to lose graciously.

## 8.2 The First Welfare Theorem

Chapter 6 discussed taking a normative approach to social decisions and how hard it is to aggregate preferences. It also defined the notion of Pareto optimality, which circumvents conceptually difficult problems and makes do with a minimal condition, roughly, that we won't be able to make everyone better off. Chapter 7 discussed a more descriptive approach and said that even Pareto optimality is not so trivial to achieve. The prisoner's dilemma was given as an example of a failure of individual rationality to lead to a Pareto-efficient outcome; and the same can happen in pure coordination games as well as in games (such as "stag hunt"), in which the Pareto-superior equilibrium is risk-dominated by a Pareto-dominated one.

In light of all these failures, it is surprising that there is some good news, however limited. The good news is that under certain conditions free markets give rise to equilibria that are Pareto-efficient. The basic conditions needed for equilibria of free markets to be Pareto-efficient are the following.

• Consumers are rational (in the classic sense). Each consumer can be thought of as maximizing a utility function given a budget constraint. Consumer preferences are fixed. In particular, consumers are not prone to be tempted by short-run considerations and to regret their choices later on.

• All products are private goods, and there are no externalities. A given unit of a product can only be consumed by one consumer, and it does not affect the others.

• Consumers prefer more to less. They may be satiated with some products but not with all of them. Thus, consumers are never left with unused income.

• Firms are rational. Each firm can be thought of as maximizing its profit given its technology and market prices.

• Both consumers and firms are price takers. They do not take into account their possible impact on market prices.

• Markets are complete. Every product—good, service, or right that affects preferences—can be traded.

• Information is shared by all agents in the market. Uncertainty might exist, but information is symmetric; no one knows more than another.

A *competitive equilibrium* is defined by prices that clear the markets. What this means is the following. We are given an economy defined by consumers' preferences, firms' technologies, and initial endowments of the consumers, both of products and of the firms' shares. All consumers are endowed with 24 hours of leisure. Some may own land or other resources. And some may own the firms, either directly or through the stock market. For such an economy, we ask whether a list of prices, one for each product, can represent an equilibrium.

Consider a suggested list of prices. To see if it is an equilibrium, we first solve the profit maximization problem for each firm. This determines the supply of products by the firms. The profits of the firms are distributed among the consumers based on the shares, which specify how much of each firm is owned by each consumer. Then we use the prices to translate the consumers' initial endowments to money. For each consumer we sum up the income from the two sources (firms' profits and initial endowment value) and treat it as income defining the budget constraint. If we now solve the consumer's problem for each consumer, we will get the consumers' demand. The prices we started out with constitute an equilibrium if in each market we find that demand equals supply or possibly exceeds it in case the price is zero.

Under these assumptions, the *first welfare theorem* states that competitive equilibria define production schedules for the firms and allocations of products among the consumers that are Pareto-optimal. That is, there is no way to suggest other production schedules and allocations that would make all consumers as well off, and some strictly better off, than at the equilibrium allocation.

The first welfare theorem relies on a simple and powerful tool: all agents in the market are optimizing *relative to the same prices*. This is the reason that they jointly compute a Pareto-optimal allocation. Let us look at a few examples that illustrate why, responding to the same prices, the agents find optimal solutions to three types of questions: (1) how much to produce of each product, (2) who should produce it, and (3) who should consume it.

Let's start with the production question. Suppose you have a leaking pipe, and there is a plumber who can fix it for you. Will it be optimal that the plumber come to fix your pipe, or should you learn to live with the leak? This is a production question. We may think of the plumber as a firm, which has a technology that allows it to convert the plumber's time into the product (service) of a fixed pipe.

Clearly, if you offer the plumber no compensation, he would not perform the job. The plumber demands compensation in terms of a fee. He will work only if he gets paid this fee (or more). You prefer the pipe to be fixed, and we assume that you are willing to pay a certain amount for the service. Let's call this amount your *reservation price*. You will hire a plumber provided that you don't have to pay more than this price. For simplicity, assume that you and the plumber are the only two individuals in the economy or that there are many identical plumbers and many consumers, all identical to you.

The question is whether your reservation price exceeds the plumber's fee. If the former is greater than the latter, that is, you are willing to pay more than the plumber demands, Pareto optimality requires that trade take place. Specifically, if you don't trade, one can find a Pareto improvement by asking the plumber to fix your pipe and asking you to pay him any amount that is above his fee and below your reservation price. Any such amount will make you both better off and will thus be a Pareto improvement relative to the original allocation.

If, however, your reservation price is below the plumber's fee, it will be Pareto-optimal for you to keep your money and get used to the leak. There is no way to have a Pareto improvement by fixing your pipe because the minimum amount required to compensate the plumber is higher than the maximum amount you are willing to pay.

Let us now see where the equilibrium price (fee) might lie, relative to the plumber's fee and your reservation price. Let's start with the second case. Your reservation price falls below the plumber's fee, so no price will be simultaneously high enough for the plumber to sell his time and low enough for you to buy it. Hence, when both you and the plumber react optimally to the same market price, whatever that price is, there will be no trade, as Pareto optimality dictates.

Now assume that your reservation price is higher than the plumber's fee. We need to be convinced that the equilibrium price will indeed be in between the two. If the price is below the plumber's fee, it is also below your reservation price. Hence you wish to hire a plumber, that is, there is demand in the labor market. But the plumber is not willing to offer labor because the price is lower than his fee. Hence, there is excess demand in the labor market, and the market is not at an equilibrium. You may expect the price to rise in this case. While this is intuitive, we do not discuss convergence to equilibrium here. It suffices that we convince ourselves that there is excess demand, which means that the market is not at an equilibrium.

Next assume that the equilibrium price is above your reservation price. Hence it is also above the plumber's fee. The plumber therefore offers his services on the labor market. But because the price is so high, you are not buying labor. The plumber doesn't get to work. The labor market will have excess supply. And this is impossible at equilibrium unless the price is zero (whereas we assumed it was high). Again, this excess supply will probably result in a lower price, but the main point is that this is not an equilibrium.

Thus we are left with the conclusion that the equilibrium price has to be between the plumber's fee and your reservation price (still assuming the latter is higher than the former). In this case, trade will take place. The plumber's optimal response to the price is to sell his time, and your optimal response is to buy it. Importantly, this is so because both of you are reacting to the same price. And trade will take place, as dictated by Pareto optimality in this case.

It is important to emphasize that the solution need not be just or fair in any way. It is possible that the plumber doesn't like his job and that he has to fix pipes because he never had a fair chance to acquire skills for jobs that he would have liked better. It is also possible that you are not paying enough for the hard job that he performs for you. All that the equilibrium guarantees is Pareto optimality. If, at equilibrium, there is no trade, say, because the plumber's fee is higher than your reservation price, you can at least rest assured that it is impossible to make both you and the plumber better off. And this is true also if, at equilibrium, trade does take place. That is, whether the equilibrium involves trade or not, no Pareto improvement is possible.

Let us turn to the second question, namely, who should produce the products. Consider the market for desks. There are different carpenters who can produce desks at different costs. Let us consider two of them,

*A* and *B*. *A* can produce a desk at a marginal cost of $200. That is, *A*'s overall expenses, including labor, raw materials, and so forth will go up by $200 if *A* decides to produce one additional desk. *B* can produce a desk at a marginal cost of $300. A production schedule that will clearly not be Pareto-optimal is one in which *B* produces a desk while *A* doesn't. Indeed, in such a case a Pareto improvement would be for *B* to subcontract the production of the desk. Rather than spending $300 on its production, *A* can do it for *B* at a cost of $200, and they can split the savings of $100 to their mutual benefit. The buyer who buys the desk from *B* will still get her desk, while the two carpenters are strictly better off. Thus we have a Pareto improvement.

However, there is no competitive equilibrium at which *B* produces the desk and *A* doesn't. If the price is below $200, neither of them will decide to produce. If the price is above $300, both will. And if the price is between $200 and $300, *A* will decide to produce and *B* won't. Because both react to the same price, the equilibrium finds a Pareto-efficient allocation of labor.

Similar logic applies to the supply of the plumber's services. If there is another plumber who can fix the pipe at a lower cost, Pareto optimality demands that the lower-cost plumber do the job. Indeed, for any market price of labor (that is, for any fee), we will find the higher-cost plumber performing the job only if the lower-cost plumber is also hired.

In both examples, the division of labor is Pareto-optimal but perhaps not fair. It is possible that the lower-cost manufacturer of the desk employs children in a developing country. Or that the lower-cost plumber can't feed his own children and is therefore willing to work for lower fees. An allocation that is Pareto-optimal is not guaranteed to be just or fair. All we know is that, if we start with such an allocation, we can't make everyone better off.

Finally, let us turn to the question of the allocation of products among the consumers. Suppose that both you and I have leaking pipes. You are willing to pay up to $100 to get your pipe fixed. I am not that rich, and I'm willing to pay only up to $50 to get my pipe fixed. Pareto optimality allows for allocations in which we both fix our pipes, allocations in which neither of us does, and allocations in which you fix your pipe and I don't fix mine. But Pareto optimality rules out a situation in which I fix my pipe and you don't. Indeed, in such a situation we can offer a Pareto improvement. I'll ask the plumber to fix your pipe instead of mine. You are willing to pay $100 for fixing your pipe, and I am indifferent between enjoying a fixed pipe and keeping my $50. Since the service is worth to you more than it is worth to me, we can split the difference, evenly or not, and both of us will be better off.

We argue that at a competitive equilibrium we will not find the Pareto-dominated allocation, in which I hire a plumber and you don't. If the market price (fee) is below $50, both of us will hire plumbers. If the price is above $100, neither will. And if the price is between these two, you will get your pipe fixed and I won't. Since we are reacting to the same market price, the Pareto-inefficient allocation will not result at equilibrium.

It is worth reiterating that no claim to fairness or justice is made here. It is possible that I'm willing to spend only $50 on fixing the leak because I spend most of my meager salary on medication for my children, and I don't have enough money left to fix pipes, whereas you are rich and healthy and can afford to spend more on leaking pipes. Still, to get my pipe fixed we will have to leave yours leaking, and this is not a Pareto improvement.

The beauty of the first welfare theorem is that if everyone is reacting optimally *to the same prices*, they are also reacting optimally to each other. In this sense, competitive equilibria suggest a huge simplification of the market problem. Imagine that we are in Moscow in 1924, and we plan how to run the economy of the USSR. We are communists, and we don't believe in free markets. But we do recognize that people have preferences and that firms have technologies, and therefore the notion of Pareto optimality makes sense to us. We can define Pareto optimality, and we have no reason not to seek it. But how would we do it? What should the production schedule be, and what should the consumption of each individual be, so that Pareto optimality will be guaranteed? We would need to ask people for their preferences, and firms for their technologies, and hope that we get truthful answers. Indeed, we have come to question the possibility of truth telling as an equilibrium. But even if we assume that people tell us the truth, we have an immensely complex computational problem. Instead, the first welfare theorem suggests that we endow people with private ownership, post a price for each product, and let everyone optimize relative to these prices. Suppose there is a market maker who adjusts the prices according to excess demand or excess supply and somehow finds prices that constitute a competitive equilibrium. Then we know that we have achieved Pareto optimality. We do not need to ask people about their preferences or firms about their technology. No one has the chance or the incentive to misrepresent anything. And we need not solve a complex problem. It is as if we had used a super-computer for the solution, where each agent in the economy is a processor, assigned to solve a small subproblem of the big social problem. Thus, free markets can be viewed as decentralizing the decision process while guaranteeing a Pareto-efficient result.

The emphasis on the assumption that all agents react to the same prices suggests that when different agents in the economy face different prices, we should be concerned. As mentioned, this is what happens in the case of taxation. This is also what happens when agents get subsidies or discounts. Typically, interventions in market operations result in situations in which different agents react to different prices, and Pareto optimality is not achieved.

### 8.3 Limitations of Free Markets

There are many reasons that the first welfare theorem might not hold or might not be very meaningful. Some of the main ones are the following.

#### 8.3.1 Externalities and Public Goods

One of the first assumptions I mentioned was that consumers only enjoy their own private goods. When public goods are involved (such as hospitals, parks, schools, and roads), the analysis changes. Typically, in such situations the contribution to the provision of the public good generates a strategic situation similar to the prisoner's dilemma; each one would prefer to contribute less, no matter what the others are contributing, even though everyone would prefer everyone to contribute rather than not to contribute. Some public goods have to do with the environment and with natural resources. For example, there is an optimal rate of fishing, which allows the fish population to renew itself. But since the payoff to each fisherman does not reflect the impact he has on others, the fishermen as a group will overfish.

There are also externalities involving the direct effect of one individual's economic activity on others. For example, smoking pollutes the air for people around us; drunken driving endangers others as well as ourselves; renovating a house has a positive effect on the entire neighborhood; and so forth. In all these examples, the individual making the decision does not take into account the overall impact of her choices.

Some of these problems can be viewed as problems of incomplete markets. For example, had there been markets in which one could trade air pollution, or if one could pay other drivers so that they wouldn't drink and drive, the externalities would have been "internalized" and we could hope that free trade would result in a Pareto-optimal outcome. But in many situations this is impractical, and often the only solution is to regulate economic behavior by law.

### 8.3.2  Market Power

A clear violation of the assumptions of competitive equilibrium occurs when some agents are large enough to have market power, namely, to affect prices in a non-negligible way. For example, if a firm is a monopolist, it obviously has an effect on prices. It will typically decide to sell less than it would in a competitive market. At a competitive equilibrium, the firm is supposed to ignore whatever effect it has on prices, and its decision whether to offer another unit of the product depends only on the comparison between the market price and the marginal production cost. But if the firm is a monopolist, it may decide not to produce the next unit—despite the fact that its cost of production is below market price—for fear of losing money on the units already sold. The same logic applies to several agents, whether on the buying or selling side of a market. The conclusion that equilibria are efficient relies on the fact that no one believes they can change market prices.

### 8.3.3  Asymmetric Information

**Lemons**  A stunning example of failure of markets was provided in 1970 by George Akerlof.[1] He suggested a stylized market for used cars. The cars can be good ("plums") or bad ("lemons"). The seller knows the quality of his car, but the buyer does not. Suppose there is demand and supply of both good and bad cars. Say, for lemons there are potential buyers who are willing to pay $6,000 and sellers who are willing to sell at $5,000. Plums can be traded at double these prices; sellers offer them as soon as the price is above $10,000, and buyers exist as long as the price does not exceed $12,000.

If the quality of a car were known to all, lemons would trade between $5,000 and $6,000, plums between $10,000 and $12,000, and all would be fine. If, on the other hand, no one knows what a car's quality is, and everyone has the same information, trade would still take place. Suppose that the cars are lemons or plums with equal probability and that the buyers and sellers are expected value maximizers. Then the sellers would sell something that is worth to them, in expectation, $7,500, and the buyers would get something that is worth to them, in expectation, $9,000. If the price were between $7,500 and $9,000, trade would take place. Indeed, this is the range where the equilibrium price should be, and Pareto optimality would hold. This would be similar to trading shares in the stock market, under the assumption that everyone has the same information.

But in Akerlof's story, information is asymmetric. The seller knows the quality of the car. The buyer doesn't, and she has to compute the expected value. She is therefore willing to pay only $9,000. Given that, sellers of good cars, who are willing to sell at $10,000 and up, will stay out of the market. As a result, only low-quality cars (lemons) will be traded in the market.

If we have many intermediate quality levels, the result will be even more striking. Top-quality cars will not be traded because sellers won't be interested in selling their great cars at the average price. Once they are out of the market, the average quality of cars goes down, and buyers are willing to pay even less than before. Then the next-to-top level drops out, and on it goes. We are left with a market in which only lemons are traded, even though Pareto optimality demands that trade take place at all quality levels.

In a sense, one can think of asymmetric information as a type of externality. The top-quality car sellers cannot distinguish themselves from the lower-quality ones. The existence of the latter is a type of externality on the former.

**Adverse Selection**   Situations of asymmetric information abound. Consider health insurance. I approach an insurance company and ask to buy a policy. They try to assess the risk involved and to price the policy accordingly. They may ask me a few questions about my health, but they are bound to know less about my health than I do. Thus, we have asymmetric information in this case.

In order not to lose money, the insurance company should price the policy a bit above the average cost. Since this is an average over healthier and less healthy clients, the healthy ones might find the cost too high for the risks they are exposed to. If they decide not to buy the insurance, the pool of clients will become worse in the sense of the expected claims. The insurance company will have to increase the premium, and the next tier of clients will also decide that this is too expensive for them and will drop out as well. The equilibrium of this process will be arrived at when the least healthy clients are insured at a very high price and the rest can't find insurance at a fair price. Again, the problem is that healthy clients can't distinguish themselves in a credible way from the less healthy ones.

This phenomenon is known in the insurance literature as *adverse selection*. By the nature of the market, the insurance companies get a selection of clients that comprises, on average, the more expensive (less healthy) ones.

**Moral Hazard and Principal Agent Problems**  Another problem of asymmetric information that arises in the context of insurance is called *moral hazard*. The problem here is that the probability of damage might also depend on precautionary measures that the client might or might not take. For example, suppose that my car is fully insured and that I stop to buy a newspaper at a newsstand. It is convenient to leave the engine running and just hop out for a second. This, however, involves the risk of the car's being stolen. If it were not insured, I might have decided to take the trouble of turning off the engine and locking the car. But because the car is insured, it is as if I were driving the insurance company's car. Hence I may be somewhat less careful with it.

Moral hazard problems occur in a variety of situations referred to as *principal agent* problems. In these problems, the principal is hiring the agent to perform a job for her, but she can't monitor the level of effort exerted by the agent. For instance, the insurance company is the principal who may or may not bear the cost of the stolen car, and the client is the agent who can affect the probability of theft by the amount of effort exerted. There are many other situations of the principal agent type. When you consult a physician or a lawyer, you hire an expert, often without being able to judge the quality of the service you get. It is not always obvious that the incentives of these professionals are fully aligned with yours. In all these cases, we have reason to doubt that free markets yield Pareto-optimal equilibria.

### 8.3.4  Existence versus Convergence

In the early 1950s, Kenneth Arrow and Gérard Debreu proved that under certain assumptions, competitive equilibria exist.[2] The assumptions include those of the first welfare theorem but also a few more, notably convexity of preferences and of technology. The proof, like the proof of existence of Nash equilibria, is not constructive, and it does not tell us how to find such equilibria. Moreover, we do not know of a dynamic process that could be thought of as a reasonable model of an economic process and that is guaranteed to converge to such equilibria.

The term *equilibrium* is borrowed from the natural sciences, and it invokes the connotation of balance between opposing forces. But since we do not have general convergence results, even if we agree with the assumptions of the model, there is no guarantee that what we observe in reality corresponds to an equilibrium.

If we take into account various external shocks that economic systems undergo, from political events to technological improvements, it becomes even less clear that the economy is at a general equilibrium. Clearly, if we are not necessarily at equilibrium, the fact that equilibria are Pareto-efficient is not very relevant.

### 8.3.5 Formation of Preference
The general equilibrium model assumes that preferences are fixed, given as part of the description of the economy. But we know that preferences are subject to change. In a sense, marketing is all about changing preferences. Preferences are affected by habits, social norms, and so forth. Of particular interest is the formation of preferences by consumption. It is often argued that we observe a process of consumerism, by which large corporations convince consumers that they have more needs, in terms of type and quantity, than they really do. If such a process in taking place, the notion of Pareto efficiency is ill-defined. The fact that consumers are willing to buy something does not mean that they really need it or that they would have missed it if it didn't exist in the market.

It seems obvious that to some extent consumers' needs are determined by economic activity. Also, much of what is provided by the market would have been needed anyway, whether food, clothes, medication, or even less basic needs. It is complicated to draw the line between needs that the market only satisfies and those that it also generates.

### 8.3.6 Irrational Behavior
Another difficulty with the first welfare theorem is that it assumes that consumers are rational in the sense of maximizing a utility function given their budget constraint. Rationality is only a model and should not be taken literally. Often it is a good enough approximation and

thus can be a useful model. But there are exceptions. For example, there is ample evidence that people tend to be myopic in their behavior in the credit market. People often incur debt that they later regret having taken on, and feel that they should have known better. Just as a person might say that he drank too much at a party, or that he smokes more than he would like, he might say, "I wish I hadn't borrowed so much money on my credit card."

Often people find that they owe credit card companies amounts that exceed their monthly income, amounts that represent the accumulation of small daily purchases. In such cases one can ask whether the utility maximization model is a good description of consumer behavior. And if it isn't, because people are too often tempted to go into debt, the image of the sovereign consumer is shaken. In particular, if people systematically make decisions they are going to regret, it is not obvious which preference relation we wish to use for the definition of Pareto optimality. And there is even room for paternalism and for restricting consumer freedom. Having more options could be a great thing for a classically rational consumer, who would never change his mind about the choices he made. But more options can also mean a trap for a consumer who behaves today in a way he will regret tomorrow.

### 8.3.7 What Is Measured by *Utility*?
The meaning of *utility* is discussed in chapter 10. Here I only mention that the implications of the first welfare theorem in everyday economic and political debate should not automatically equate utility with well-being. Thus, achieving Pareto optimality with respect to the preference relations of consumers need not mean exactly what we would like it to mean.

### 8.3.8 A Limitation of Pareto Optimality
Finally, recall that Pareto optimality is a limited concept and that, in particular, it says nothing about equality. The theory has a partial response to this, in the form of the second welfare theorem. This theorem states that under certain assumptions (including convexity of preferences and of technologies), *any* Pareto-efficient outcome can be a competitive equilibrium, provided we make certain transfers before production and trade begin. That is, given a Pareto-efficient outcome, we can change the initial endowments and find that the given outcome is an equilibrium of the modified economy, in which preferences and technologies are unchanged. Such transfers are called *lump-sum trans-*

*fers,* which are supposed to be independent of economic activity. In contrast to taxes on income and on consumption, lump-sum transfers do not change incentives because the amount one yields or receives (of each product and each share) is not affected by one's economic decisions.

The idea of the second welfare theorem could be described as saying that if one is concerned about inequality, one could fix this problem by lump-sum transfers without sacrificing Pareto efficiency. Presumably, equality could be achieved by a reallocation of initial resources alone, without tampering with the workings of the free market. The problem is that we have no examples of lump-sum transfers that appear reasonable. For instance, transferring products among people according to their names doesn't sound fair and will not solve problems of inequality. If, by contrast, we transfer resources from the rich to the poor, people will soon realize this, and such transfers will be similar to an income tax. As a result, the second welfare theorem is of limited practical value.

## 8.4 Example

The debate about the pros and cons of free markets is very active. The first welfare theorem is probably the most powerful result in economics from a rhetorical viewpoint. It also has a claim to be the most overinterpreted and misunderstood result in the field. As such, it deserves to have a long list of qualifications. At the same time, it is important to understand the basic logic of the first welfare theorem. Even if we do not automatically adopt its conclusion when it comes to whole economies, it is an insight that can help us allocate resources efficiently. Consider the following example.

Students select courses at a university. Classes are limited in size, and therefore the students can't always get their first choices. How should we allocate the students to the courses? If we choose a random assignment, we have very little hope of getting a Pareto-efficient allocation. For example, we may assign one student to a morning section and another to an evening section of the same course, when in fact they would have liked to switch. In order to find the Pareto-improving trade, we could match any pair of students and let them find out if there is a reallocation of their courses that would make them both happier. Matching any two students will be a very lengthy process. Worse still, it might not suffice. It is possible that only a three-way exchange will leave all the students better off, and we won't find these by pair-wise comparisons. And if we need to consider all subsets of students, this will be even more complicated.

The first welfare theorem offers a way out. Allocate to each student a budget of, say, 100 points. Post prices per courses (or sections), and let the students buy the right to register for a course with their points. Given the prices posted, the students can also trade with each other. Let a market maker adjust the posted prices based on supply and demand of slots for each course at the given prices. If the market maker arrived at an equilibrium, we know that it is Pareto-efficient.

Many universities employ bidding systems whereby course allocation is done by auctions in which points are used to bid for course registration. An auction mechanism may not guarantee Pareto-optimal outcomes, but it has the advantage of being implementable in a relatively short time.

Another alternative to the trade in points is the first come, first served system. It may be viewed as a market system where consumers pay with time; the student who arrives first chooses all the courses she wants and leaves the market. The next student then chooses his courses, and so forth. If there are no indifferences; the outcome of such a system will be Pareto-efficient, but it seems far from equitable. Indeed, a student who is a single parent may not be able to line up for registration as early as a childless student would. Thus, with a small time endowment a student would have fewer options than one with a large endowment.

Looking for a competitive equilibrium with points is a way to obtain a Pareto-optimal allocation that is also egalitarian in the sense that we set all endowments to be equal. In this example, most qualifications of the first welfare theorem do not seem relevant. No student has significant market power, there is no asymmetric information, and so forth. Consequently, the market mechanism appears quite attractive in this case.

This example is another instance of the theory-paradigm duality. The first welfare theorem is fraught with difficulties as a theory about real markets in entire economies. Yet, it suggests a powerful insight that may be used in other contexts.

# IV    Rationality and Emotions

# 9 Evolutionary View of Emotions

It is common to view rationality as the opposite of emotionality. Presumably, emotions are ill-explained forces that sometimes take over, whereas reason is the cool, calculating machine that helps us control our emotions.

There is surely some truth to this depiction. Consider a man who comes home, finds his wife in bed with another man, pulls out a gun, shoots them both to death, and spends the rest of his life in jail. The man might well regret his choice and say that he "lost his reason," that "emotion took over," and the like. Indeed, this might qualify as a "crime of passion." Undoubtedly, the man could have thought better. Instead of pulling the trigger, he would have been better off shrugging his shoulders and going to the bar in search of a new partner.

But this is not the case with all emotional reactions. On the contrary, many emotions could be viewed as determinants of utility that make sense from an evolutionary point of view. For example, people tend to love their children. This is manifested by the parents' willingness to consume less of available resources so that their children can consume more. This might not appear rational if one believes that the sole determinants of utility are physical needs. But it does make sense if one incorporates the physical needs of the loved one into the utility function. Moreover, it is easy to see that preferences that reflect love might be developed in an evolutionary process. If two species are equal in all respects except for love of their offspring, one can imagine that the selfish parents will have, on average, fewer children reaching adulthood than the parents who care for their children. One might wonder whether it makes sense for a parent to sacrifice his or her life in order to save the child's life. Evolutionary calculations here might depend on the precise model. But there is no doubt that giving up a little bit of

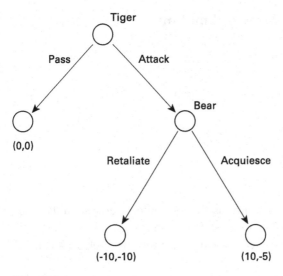

Figure 9.1

material well-being in order to provide for the child makes evolutionary sense.

An emotion such as anger can also be explained on evolutionary
grounds. Consider the following extensive form game between a tiger
and a she-bear (see figure 9.1). The she-bear goes off to get food for her
cubs, whom she leaves behind. The tiger stops by, smells the alluring
meal, and has to decide whether to attack the cubs or not. If the tiger
passes, nothing happens, and we can normalize the payoffs to be $(0,0)$
for the tiger and the she-bear, respectively. Should the tiger attack the
cubs, he'll stay to eat. Suppose, for simplicity, that he will kill them all
and that the she-bear will be back before the meal is over. Now she has
a choice of fighting the tiger or not. If she fights, both she and the tiger
will be hurt, and the payoff is, say, $(-10, -10)$. If she decides to go on
without fighting, the tiger will have had a great meal, and she will lose
her cubs but at least not get hurt. Assume that payoff is $(10, -5)$.

The game has two pure strategy Nash equilibria. In the first, the
tiger attacks and the she-bear walks away (Acquiesce), muttering to
herself, "Let bygones be bygones," resulting in the payoff $(10, -5)$.
This is the best outcome for the tiger, and attacking is definitely his
best response to the she-bear's choice of acquiescence. As far as the
she-bear is concerned, it's better to lose the cubs $(-5)$ then to lose
the cubs *and* to get hurt $(-10)$. Hence, acquiescence is a best response to

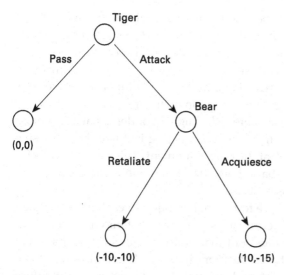

**Figure 9.2**

the tiger's choice of attacking. In the second equilibrium, the she-bear chooses to retaliate in case her cubs are eaten. Given this choice, the tiger's best response is to give up on the meal (Pass). The she-bear's threat of fighting is a best response to the tiger's choice of passing because the threat never gets to be implemented. Indeed, the first equilibrium is subgame perfect, and the second one isn't. In fact, this game is very similar to the hand grenade game discussed in section 7.7. The equilibrium that is not subgame perfect is hardly reasonable as a result of an evolutionary process. If, once in a blue moon, the tiger mistakenly attacks the cubs, the rational she-bear will not follow the noncredible threat. The tiger will then find out that the threat of retaliation was empty.

Let us now endow the she-bear with anger. Suppose that upon finding her dead cubs, she is consumed with rage, and she just cannot help but fight the tiger. This could be modeled by changing the payoff of $-5$ to $-15$; acquiescing is now worse than retaliating. Recall that utility describes behavior; the inequality $-15 < -10$ describes the she-bear's choice of fighting. The new game is shown in figure 9.2.

If we analyze the new game, we find it is similar to the gun game of section 7.7. The game has only one pure Nash equilibrium. It is subgame perfect and equal to the backward induction solution. The she-bear credibly threatens to fight if her cubs are attacked. The tiger chooses to pass.

Anger thus made the she-bear's threat credible. A species of bears with anger as an emotion might, from time to time, lose its cubs and get hurt fighting. But it will have a reputation of a species tigers should be careful with. Tigers will tend not to attack such cubs, and this species will have more cubs reaching adulthood. Evolution will favor this species, thereby selecting for the emotion of anger.

The story may not end there. We might wonder what prevents a particular she-bear from free-riding, appearing just like the other she-bears but failing to attack at the crucial moment. This question calls for further analysis. But the basic point stands: emotions can change payoffs in a way that increases fitness.

Neurological studies have found that emotional reactions are related to rational decisions. Neurologists such as Antonio Damasio and Joseph LeDoux have pointed out that brain studies suggest that emotions are needed for rational decision making.[1] Taking a purely theoretical perspective, we also find the ability to reason does not suffice for rational choice. Pure reason may suffice to solve mathematical problems, but if we do not have likes and dislikes, we will not be able to decide what to do. Affective responses, having to do with emotions, feelings, or moods, are needed to define wants and desires. If you show me a model of a game, I may be very smart and find all its equilibria, but if I do not know which utility function I should maximize, I will have no way to make a choice.

We conclude that to a large extent rationality is compatible with emotions. Moreover, rationality can help us understand emotions, and vice versa. On the one hand, an evolutionary perspective often suggests that it is rational to have emotional reactions. On the other hand, emotional reactions are necessary for the definition of rational choice.

# 10 Utility and Well-Being

## 10.1 Money Isn't Happiness

It is very natural to identify the notion of utility with such concepts as well-being or even happiness. One may even argue that this is what utility is supposed to measure. But it does not follow from anything said previously that this is what it does in fact measure.

Utility was defined by the way we use it. In choice under certainty, maximization of utility described choices made by individuals who are consistent enough in their behavior to admit such a representation. The same was true of maximization of expected utility in the context of choices under risk or under uncertainty (with subjective probabilities). The function used to describe behavior can be used for prediction, and it was named a utility function. Yet, thinking of it as well-being or as happiness might be unwarranted.

It is obvious that what makes people happy, satisfied, or content has to do with various factors that may evade the measurement of utility by choices. Whether one is content or not depends not only on the alternatives available but also on aspirations, expectations, and reference points. These benchmarks depend on culture, on the society in which the individual lives, on her past, and so on.

There is ample evidence that people's self-reported (subjective) well-being is only weakly correlated with income. Famous studies by Richard Easterlin (starting in the 1970s) showed that an increase in income had very little effect on improvement in reported well-being.[1] The correlation between income and well-being within a cohort tends to be much higher than across time, and this is typically interpreted as the effect of adjustment of the aspiration level. Assume that reported well-being is the difference between one's income and one's aspiration level. Over the course of a lifetime, an individual may well become wealthier, but her aspiration level may go up as well. Hence, the difference between the two need not increase. By contrast, in a given cohort, when people look around to see how well others are doing, they all observe the same population, and as a result they have similar aspiration levels. This means that higher income will result in higher well-being when measured in the same cohort. Taken together, these findings suggest that subjective well-being depends on wealth as well as on aspirations.

The notion of a reference point that serves as a benchmark, as the aspiration level does in the context of income, appears in psychology in different guises.[2] Harry Helson (starting in the 1940s) developed adaptation level theory,[3] which models perception of various stimuli by their differences from a certain level, which is adapted as a result of experiences. For example, when we are in the dark, our pupils enlarge until we get used to the given level of light. Walking into a kitchen, you might be struck by the smell of cooking, which you won't notice after a few minutes. Our minds seem to respond mostly to *changes* in levels of stimuli rather than to the absolute values of these stimuli. This makes sense because the changes tend to contain new pieces of information.

Helson's adaptation level theory was applied, among other things, to the notion of well-being. It has been argued that people adjust to life circumstances in the same way as they adjust to perceptual stimuli. A famous study by Brickman, Coates, and Janoff-Bulman (in the 1970s) measured reported well-being of people who won lotteries, on the one hand, and of people who were crippled in accidents, on the other.[4] The finding was that immediately after the event, reported well-being changed, as one would expect, but that after a while it changed back almost to its original level.

Given these findings, one might rethink the notion of welfare. If people anyway adapt to new circumstances, what is the point in pursuing material well-being? If the rich are no happier than the poor, does it make sense to measure the success of nations and economies by the Gross Domestic Product (GDP)? Is it wise to design social and economic policies with this measure in mind? To be more concrete, should we take the United States as a model of a successful economy, or should we rather prefer a developing country, where people have more leisure and put a greater emphasis on social relationships than on income?

## 10.2  Qualifications

The basic fact that money can't buy happiness is obvious. It is to be found in stories and fables, sermons and movies. Yet, it is not obvious how we should interpret the findings from the subjective well-being literature and how we should change our social and economic policies in their light.

### 10.2.1  The Validity of Questionnaires

In light of the findings that income is only weakly correlated with well-being, economists often resort to the meaning of utility as predicting choice (the "revealed preference" paradigm), and ask, at the end of the day, would you prefer to have more or less? In particular, the findings of Brickman, Coates, and Janoff-Bulman are considered suspicious. We may accept the fact that the reported well-being of paraplegics and lottery winners were found similar a while after the event. But economists often point out that, given the choice between winning the lottery and becoming crippled, no one would be even close to indifference. It is suggested that despite the problems just mentioned, the utility function used to describe choices is more meaningful, even when interpreted as a measure of well-being, than the replies to questionnaires.

This view is supported by criticism of subjective measures of well-being from the psychological literature. Two famous examples illustrate the point. In the first,[5] students were asked on the same questionnaire, How satisfied are you with your life? and How many dates have you had over the past month? When the questions were given in this order, the correlation between the replies was not too high. This might indicate that one's romantic life doesn't have a very large effect on one's well-being. But when the order of the questions was reversed, the correlation rose dramatically, suggesting the opposite conclusion. Taken together, the two findings indicate that the answers to self-report questions about well-being can be manipulated by drawing the person's attention to particular aspects of his life. Note that the question about the number of dates is a factual one and therefore less likely to be manipulable. By contrast, it makes sense that the subjective experience of well-being depends on mood, which can easily be changed if we are reminded of a certain aspect of our lives.

The second famous example involved a phone questionnaire conducted in the morning hours in various towns.[6] First, people were asked how satisfied they were with their lives, and the replies were found to be highly correlated with the weather in their town that morning. This finding suggests that waking up to a grey sky has a negative effect on one's notion of well-being, whereas a bright day makes us feel generally happier. Next, the same study was run again, but this time the respondents were first asked what the weather was like in their town. Interestingly, the correlation between the weather and the self-reported well-being dropped significantly. That is, people seemed to be able to "deduct" the effect of the weather on their mood when the weather was pointed out to them.

The first example shows that subjective well-being, as measured by self-report questionnaires, in highly manipulable. The second shows that people are actually sophisticated enough to be able to correct for transient effects when these are made explicit. But both examples suggest that the self-report measures might give very different results, depending on a variety of factors we do not deem essential. If the replies to such questions are so sensitive, it is not clear that we wish to base social and economic policies on them.

Daniel Kahneman launched a project that would allow a better measurement of well-being than subjective reports on the one hand or income on the other.[7] It is based on the Day Reconstruction Method, by which people are asked to reconstruct their day, and their well-being is measured as an integral, over time, of the activities they engaged in; the activities are separately rated for pleasurability.

Both subjective well-being and the Day Reconstruction Method do not target notions of happiness as expressed in everyday parlance and in popular culture. For example, the subjective well-being of people with no children is reportedly higher than that of people with children when the children are young but about the same when the children are grown.[8] Does that mean that people without children are happier? This is not obvious. It is quite possible that parents of young children are stressed out, find themselves struggling with too little time and too little money, and therefore their reported well-being is lower than that of people without children. The Day Reconstruction Method will probably yield similar results. Compared to childless adults, parents will have more sleepless nights, spend more time taking their children to the doctor, and go out less to entertainment in the evenings. At the same time, parents would say that their children bring happiness and joy into their lives. These notions may not be captured by existing measures, and yet they seem to be important determinants of happiness and well-being. Indeed, they also seem to affect people's choices.

Similarly, people often think of various achievements that "give meaning to their lives," "make them happy," "make their lives worth living." These can range from personal feats such as winning an Olympic medal or creating a piece of art to living a righteous life or serving one's nation. Existing measures of well-being do not seem to reflect these factors. Yet, the latter can have an effect on people's well-being as well as on their choices and on the recommendations they would give to others.

### 10.2.2 Don't Push Others off the Hedonic Treadmill

Based on adaptation level theory, Philip Brickman and Donald Campbell (in the 1970s) argued that "there is no true solution to the problem of happiness" except "getting off the Hedonic Treadmill."[9] In their view, our quest for happiness through material achievements is akin to a rodent who is running on a treadmill; the faster it runs, the faster the steps drop beneath it. Just like the animal who can't climb up, a person who seeks greater material good will not achieve happiness because his goals and aspirations rise with his success.

The "hedonic treadmill" is a powerful metaphor, and many of us may decide to adopt Brickman and Campbell's recommendations, which are in line with the teachings of philosophers and religious preachers through the ages. But the very act of making this recommendation raises ethical issues. I may decide to step off the hedonic treadmill myself, but what gives me the right to recommend that you do it? Worse still, how would I feel if you followed my advice but the people around you did not? You may find yourself poorer than everyone around you, and some sense of envy might be unavoidable. It is possible that everyone will be better off if everyone quits the pursuit of material wealth, but given that the others are at a certain level of material wealth, each of us would be happier to have just a little bit more. This would be akin to a prisoner's dilemma, where the cooperative outcome, in which we do not engage in competition for material goods, Pareto-dominates the uncooperative one, but the latter is selected by dominant strategies. Finally, the suggestion that other people should forgo material wealth also raises a problem of a moral hazard. Are we suggesting it so that we can end up being the rich and happy ones?

### 10.2.3    People Don't Adjust to Everything

Adaptation level theory suggests that people adjust to levels of stimuli. An important point, emphasized by Daniel Kahneman among others, is that there are certain things to which people do not adjust. Deprived of food, people do not get used to their unfortunate circumstances; rather, they die. Hence it would be a mistake to assume that, generally speaking, people adjust and that we should therefore not worry about their material well-being.

Moreover, material well-being and measurable indices such as GDP evidently allow a higher level of welfare. Countries with higher GDP can fight famine and disease more effectively, provide better health care, and have lower rates of infant mortality. This suggests that in the presence of welfare policies, material well-being translates to higher subjective well-being at the lower end of the income scale. According to this view, economic growth does not maximize the happiness of the rich, but it can minimize the misery of the poor.

To conclude, we do not seem to have good measures of happiness. Moreover, it is far from obvious that "we know it when we see it." By contrast, we have a much better idea of what misery is. One possible conclusion, in line with the position of John Rawls, is that social policies should focus on the minimization of misery rather than on the maximization of happiness.

# Epilogue

The rational choice paradigm provides a way of thinking about the world, but it does not provide answers to a multitude of concrete questions. Throughout this book we have encountered questions that arise in the social sciences and that lead us to traditional questions in philosophy. Problems that range from the definition of probability to the meaning of happiness, from the notion of rationality to the essence of justice, belong to the realm of philosophy, but they pop up in practical guises in questions of the social sciences.

Most of these philosophical questions do not have objective or scientific answers. Correspondingly, many practical problems in the social sciences cannot be settled based on scientific enquiry alone, and therefore they cannot be relegated to experts. Rather, these questions should be tackled by each and every individual. I believe that the rational choice paradigm can be a powerful aid in thinking about such problems.

# Notes

## Chapter 1

1. This is related to the modern theories of reduction of cognitive dissonance. See L. Festinger, *A Theory of Cognitive Dissonance* (Stanford, Calif.: Stanford University Press, 1957).

## Chapter 3

1. This approach to mathematical models dates back to Alfred Marshall, one of the forefathers of economic analysis, who wrote in 1906, "I went more and more on the rules—(1) Use mathematics as a shorthand language, rather than an engine of inquiry. (2) Keep to them till you have done. (3) Translate into English. (4) Then illustrate by examples that are important in real life. (5) Burn the mathematics. (6) If you can't succeed in (4), burn (3). This last I did often." Quoted in S. Brue, *The Evolution of Economic Thought*, 5th ed. (Fort Worth, Tex.: Dryden Press, 1993), 294.

## Chapter 4

1. J. von Neumann and O. Morgenstern, *Theory of Games and Economic Behavior* (Princeton, N.J.: Princeton University Press, 1944).

2. Apparently, the game of Blackjack is an exception; if one can recall which cards came out during the game, one can develop strategies that guarantee positive expected gain.

3. D. Kahneman and A. Tversky, "Prospect Theory: An Analysis of Decision under Risk," *Econometrica* 47 (1979): 263–291.

4. The original formulation of prospect theory, as of vNM's theory, is in the context of risk, where probabilities are assumed to be given. Problems in which probabilities are not explicitly given are discussed later.

## Chapter 5

1. Tversky and Kahneman provided insightful examples in which people tend to violate these simple rules. See A. Tversky and D. Kahneman, "Extensional vs. Intuitive Reasoning: The Conjunction Fallacy in Probability Judgment," *Psychological Review* 90 (1983): 293–315.

2. B. de Finetti, "La prévision: ses lois logiques, ses sources subjectives," *Annales de l'Institut Henri Poincaré* 7 (1937): 1–68; L. J. Savage, *The Foundations of Statistics*, 2d rev. ed. (New York: Dover Publications, 1972).

3. D. Schmeidler, "Subjective Probability and Expected Utility without Additivity," *Econometrica* 57 (1989): 571–587; I. Gilboa and D. Schmeidler, "Maxmin Expected Utility with a Non-Unique Prior," *Journal of Mathematical Economics* 18 (1989): 141–153.

4. D. Kahneman and A. Tversky, "On the Psychology of Prediction," *Psychological Review* 80 (1973): 237–251.

5. At least, this is the standard story. For details, see P. Squire, "Why the 1936 Literary Digest Poll Failed," *Public Opinion Quarterly* 52 (1988): 125–133.

## Chapter 6

1. J. C. Harsanyi, "Cardinal Utility in Welfare Economics and in the Theory of Risk-Taking," *Journal of Political Economy* 61 (1953): 434–435; J. C. Harsanyi, "Cardinal Welfare, Individualistic Ethics, and Interpersonal Comparisons of Utility," *Journal of Political Economy* 63 (1955): 309–321; J. Rawls, *A Theory of Justice* (Cambridge, Mass.: Harvard University Press, 1971).

2. K. J. Arrow, "A Difficulty in the Concept of Social Welfare," *Journal of Political Economy* 58 (1950): 328–346.

3. In the presence of other axioms, this condition also characterizes scoring rules. See H. P. Young, "Social Choice Scoring Functions," *SIAM Journal of Applied Mathematics* 28 (1975): 824–838; R. B. Myerson, "Axiomatic Derivation of Scoring Rules without the Ordering Assumption," *Social Choice and Welfare* 12 (1995): 59–74; I. Gilboa and D. Schmeidler, "Inductive Reasoning: An Axiomatic Approach," *Econometrica* 71 (2003): 1–26.

4. S. Brams and P. Fishburn, "Approval Voting," *American Political Science Review* 72 (1978): 831–847; R. J. Weber, "Approval Voting," *The Journal of Economic Perspectives* 9 (1995): 39–49.

5. A. Gibbard, "Manipulation of Voting Schemes: A General Result," *Econometrica* 41 (1973): 587–601; M. A. Satterthwaite, "Strategy-Proofness and Arrow's Conditions: Existence and Correspondence Theorems for Voting Procedures and Social Welfare Functions," *Journal of Economic Theory* 10 (1975): 187–217.

6. See P. Mongin, "Spurious Unanimity and the Pareto Principle," paper presented at the Conference of the International Society for Utilitarian Studies (ISUS), New Orleans, 1997. This example is taken from I. Gilboa, D. Samet, and D. Schmeidler "Utilitarian Aggregation of Beliefs and Tastes," *Journal of Political Economy* 112 (2004): 932–938.

## Chapter 7

1. J. F. Nash, "Non-Cooperative Games," *Annals of Mathematics* 54 (1951): 286–295.

2. See *Immanuel Kant: The Moral Law*, translated with a preface, commentary, and analysis by H. J. Paton (London: Routledge, 1948).

3. D. Bernheim, "Rationalizable Strategic Behavior," *Econometrica* 52 (1984): 1007–1028; D. Pearce, "Rationalizable Strategic Behavior and the Problem of Perfection," *Econometrica* 52 (1984): 1029–1050.

4. J. C. Harsanyi and R. Selten, *A General Theory of Equilibrium Selection in Games* (Cambridge, Mass.: MIT Press, 1988).

5. D. K. Lewis, *Convention: A Philosophical Study* (Cambridge, Mass.: Harvard University Press, 1969); R. J. Aumann, "Agreeing to Disagree," *Annals of Statistics* 4 (1976): 1236–1239; J. Y. Halpern and Y. Moses, "Knowledge and Common Knowledge in a Distributed Environment," *Annual ACM Symposium on Principles of Distributed Computing* (New York: ACM, 1984), 50–61; R. Fagin, J. Y. Halpern, Y. Moses, and M. Y. Vardi, *Reasoning about Knowledge* (Cambridge, Mass.: MIT Press, 1995).

6. R. Selten, "Spieltheoretische Behandlung eines Oligopolmodells mit Nachftragetragheit," *Zeitschrift für die gesampte Staatswissenschaft* 121 (1965): 667–689; R. Selten, "A Reexamination of the Perfectness Concept for Equilibrium Points in Extensive Games," *International Journal of Game Theory* 4 (1975): 25–55.

7. Making this statement precise has turned out to be a rather tricky business. The vaility of this belief depends on the precise definitions of *rationality* and *common knowledge*. See R. J. Aumann, "Backward Induction and Common Knowledge of Rationality," *Games and Economic Behavior* 8 (1995): 6–19.

## Chapter 8

1. G. A. Akerlof, "The Market for 'Lemons': Quality Uncertainty and the Market Mechanism," *Quarterly Journal of Economics* 84 (1970): 488–500.

2. K. J. Arrow and G. Debreu, "Existence of an Equilibrium for a Competitive Economy," *Econometrica* 22 (1954): 265–290. The general equilibrium model is typically called the Arrow-Debreu model. Kenneth Arrow and Gérard Debreu were the first to state and prove the existence theorem. However, the model itself had precursors, and without production it had already been formulated by Leon Walras in the mid-nineteenth century.

## Chapter 9

1. A. R. Damasio, *Descartes's Error: Emotion, Reason, and the Human Brain* (New York: Putnam, 1994); J. LeDoux, *The Emotional Brain* (New York: Simon and Schuster, 1996).

## Chapter 10

1. R. A. Easterlin, "Does Money Buy Happiness?" *Public Interest* 30 (1973): 3–10; R. A. Easterlin, "Does Economic Growth Improve the Human Lot?" in *Economic Growth*, ed. P. A. David and M. W. Reder, 89–125 (New York: Academic Press, 1974); E. Diener, "Subjective Well-Being," *Psychological Bulletin* 95 (1984): 542–575. However, see also R. E. Lucas, P. S. Dyrenforth, and E. Diener, "Four Myths about Subjective Well-Being," *Social and Personality Psychology Compass* 2 (2008): 2001–2015.

2. The notion of aspiration level appears in Herbert Simon's theory of satisficing. In this theory, the aspiration level has a much more behavioral flavor; it is not a measure of happiness or well-being but rather of a performace level above which one is "satisficed" and ceases to experiment. See H. A. Simon, "A Behavioral Model of Rational Choice," *Quarterly Journal of Economics* 69 (1955): 99–118.

3. H. Helson, "Adaptation-Level as Frame of Reference for Prediction of Psychophysical Data," *American Journal of Psychology* 60 (1947): 1–29; H. Helson, "Adaptation-Level as a

Basis for a Quantitative Theory of Frames of Reference," *Psychological Review* 55 (1948): 297–313.

4. P. Brickman, D. Coates, and R. Janoff-Bulman, "Lottery Winners and Accident Victims: Is Happiness Relative?" *Journal of Personality and Social Psychology* 36 (1978): 917–927.

5. F. Strack, L. Martin, and N. Schwarz, "Priming and Communication: Social Determinants of Information Use in Judgments of Life Satisfaction." *European Journal of Social Psychology* 18 (1988): 429–442.

6. N. Schwarz and G. L. Clore, "Mood, Misattribution, and Judgments of Well-Being: Informative and Directive Functions of Affective States," *Journal of Personality and Social Psychology* 45 (1983): 513–523.

7. D. Kahneman, A. B. Krueger, D. A. Schkade, N. Schwarz, and A. A. Stone, "A Survey Method for Characterizing Daily Life Experience: The Day Reconstruction Method," *Science* 306 (2004): 1776–780.

8. S. Mcklanahan and J. Adams, "Parenthood and Psychological Well-Being," *Annual Review of Sociology* 13 (1987): 237–257; D. Umberson and W. R. Gove, "Parenthood and Psychological Well-Being: Theory, Measurement, and Stage in Family Life Course," *Journal of Family Issues* 10 (1989): 440–462.

9. P. Brickman and D. T. Campbell, "Hedonic Relativism and Planning the Good Society," in *Adaptation Level Theory: A Symposium*, ed. M. H. Appley (New York: Academic Press, 1971).

# Index

Printed in the United States
by Baker & Taylor Publisher Services

Printed in the United States
by Baker & Taylor Publisher Services